An Illustrated Guide to Clinical Psychology

of related interest

Child Trauma and Attachment in Common Sense and Doodles – Second Edition
Miriam Silver
Illustrated by Teg Lansdell
ISBN 978 1 83997 912 5
eISBN 978 1 83997 913 2

Digital Delivery of Mental Health Therapies
A Guide to the Benefits and Challenges, and Making It Work
Edited by Hannah Wilson
Foreword by John Powell
ISBN 978 1 78775 724 0
eISBN 978 1 78775 736 3

Trauma Is Really Strange
Steven Haines
Illustrated by Sophie Standing
ISBN 978 1 84819 293 5
eISBN 978 0 85701 240 1

Anxiety Is Really Strange
Steven Haines
Illustrated by Sophie Standing
ISBN 978 1 84819 389 5
eISBN 978 0 85701 345 3

Gender Is Really Strange
Teddy G. Goetz, MD, MS
Illustrated by Sophie Standing
ISBN 978 1 83997 512 7
eISBN 978 1 83997 528 8

An Illustrated Guide to
CLINICAL
PSYCHOLOGY

Dr Juliet Young, Dr Catherine Butler
*and **Dr Rachel Paskell***

Illustrated by Dr Juliet Young

Jessica Kingsley Publishers
London and Philadelphia

First published in Great Britain in 2024 by Jessica Kingsley Publishers
An imprint of John Murray Press

A CIP catalogue record for this title is available from the
British Library and the Library of Congress

ISBN 978 1 80501 004 3
eISBN 978 1 80501 005 0

2

Printed and bound by CPI Group (UK) Ltd, Croydon, CR0 4YY

Jessica Kingsley Publishers' policy is to use papers that are natural,
renewable and recyclable products and made from wood grown in
sustainable forests. The logging and manufacturing processes are expected
to conform to the environmental regulations of the country of origin.

Jessica Kingsley Publishers
Carmelite House
50 Victoria Embankment
London EC4Y 0DZ

www.jkp.com

John Murray Press
Part of Hodder & Stoughton Ltd
An Hachette Company

This book is dedicated to all those who contribute to the positive aspects and influences of clinical psychology, and the profession's ongoing learning and development. This especially includes those who share their personal experiences of mental health and wellbeing difficulties through research and/or services where clinical psychologists work. We also dedicate it to all those who have supported, guided and shaped us personally.

Acknowledgements

Anton, Iyunade, Georgia and Edward for all giving such useful feedback.

Contents

Preface

This book has been the joint effort of three UK clinical psychologists who came together to produce an accessible introduction to our profession. Much of clinical psychology's written information is dense and difficult to access for those who struggle with reading or are time-limited. This book offers a whistle-stop tour of topics we see as important or relevant to anyone wanting to know more about clinical psychology. We hope to have provided a good introduction but recognize the limitation of distilling information in this way and the risk that important nuances may be lost. Therefore, we do not consider this to be an academic text; it is not heavily laden with references and does not provide a complete overview of any area. It is a starting place and, should it spark interest, offers the reader the choice to extend their reading into more academic papers and research. All authors have contributed to the contents of the book and the topics have been illustrated to illuminate the text.

Introduction

What is clinical psychology?

Clinical psychology is the practice of applying psychological theory and research to prevent and reduce mental ill health and promote psychological wellbeing. It is a broad, diverse and eclectic discipline, which is embedded in a wide range of services and settings. Some may see clinical psychology as the practice of delivering individualized assessments, therapy or support ('interventions') in a therapy room, whereas others may see it as working with multiple systems to improve mental health and wellbeing of individuals or communities.

This book is written from the view that clinical psychology can be many things: it is about offering therapy to individuals, couples or families; about being a team member; and working with teams from different positions (e.g. leadership). It is about working to effect change on the systems that contribute to distress. It is about research and working as a reflexive scientist clinician (explained later in the book). It is also about being critical about the profession and its context and holding in mind multiple perspectives of what clinical psychology means to people.

Who is this book for?

This book can be for anyone who finds it useful. We considered the audience and particularly held in mind those early in their clinical psychology journey. This may be those just wanting to know more; those clear on their aspiration to become clinical psychologists; trainees who need an overview of new topics; and experienced psychologists who would find it helpful to be reminded about areas of their training. We think it might also be useful for other professionals and those who work with clinical psychologists to understand what clinical psychologists do and what informs this.

Language, terminology and style

The process of writing this book involved dividing up sections, with all authors reviewing and editing content. There will therefore be some differences in style and language across the topics. We have tried to write from a more narrative position to reduce the formality of academic writing, and some terminology may not suit all. We recognize that over time terminology may change, so we write using what is current to us at the time of publication.

Feedback on the book

We have attempted to gain feedback during the writing of this book and have been very grateful to those who gave their time and opinions to support its production. This is an important process but never exhaustive, and we welcome ongoing feedback from readers. The book may be updated in later versions, and critique is welcomed to challenge the content and help produce a resource that does not exclude or occlude.

About the authors and their 'stance' towards clinical psychology

When starting to write this book, the three of us reflected on our identities and how this may impact on what we chose to include. As three white women with a number of shared identities, we understood that many perspectives are lost and that content will be influenced heavily by our views on what is valuable. It is important this book is read through a critical lens: the information included comes from just three positions, and this book does not provide the totality of clinical psychology. We considered how we might address this and concluded that while we can remain critical and reflective of our writing, neutrality is not possible. Instead, we have decided to each offer a snapshot of ourselves to give the reader an understanding of some of the lenses we may be working through.

Juliet: I am a clinical psychologist (and part time illustrator) working and living in Bristol, UK. The professional experiences that influence the lens I write through include working in schools, on adult crisis teams, with care-experienced children and with young people seeking UK asylum. I have a master's in Clinical and Community Psychology from the  University of East London and a Doctorate in Clinical Psychology from the University of Bath. I now work full-time in NHS mental health services. I tend to hold a systemic lens to understanding emotional distress and am interested in community psychology approaches. I also see value in more individualistic approaches such as cognitive behavioural therapy (CBT) and am an accredited CBT therapist. I have an emerging specialist interest in trauma and NHS service development.

In terms of the identities and personal experiences that shape my writing, I primarily grew up in a close-knit Cornish community where collectivist values were centred. This provides the backdrop for many of my community psychology values and where, growing up in a single parent working class household, my work ethic was born. My class identity is muddled; I identify with and am proud of many aspects of my working class experiences growing up, but now live a middle class lifestyle. I hold multiple privileged identities including being a white, heterosexual, cisgender woman who is educated to doctoral level. I also hold some experiences of disadvantage including diagnoses of attention deficit hyperactivity disorder (ADHD), dyslexia and sensory-processing issues that have a debilitating impact across many areas of my life. I see this neurodiversity as simultaneously linked to many of my professional strengths and also the ability to visualize, understand and illustrate complex concepts that has led to the creation of this book.

Catherine: At the time of writing, I have been qualified as a clinical psychologist for 20 years and I am currently the Programme Director of the Doctorate in Clinical Psychology at the University of Exeter. I have also been qualified as a systemic psychotherapist for 18 years. I studied clinical psychology at the University of East London (UEL), which fitted with my values in addressing power imbalances and with the social-constructionist training I had started in systemic therapy. I am forever grateful to the training staff at UEL for shaping and stretching me and setting me on a path of continual learning and wanting to improve the profession to address societal power imbalances that are reflected within it.

Like Juliet, I also grew up in a single-parent household, but this was from the age of nine and prior to this we lived a middle-class life. In my teenage years, class was confusing because Margaret Thatcher's 'assisted place' scheme meant I had a scholarship to go to a private school, but I was always on the edge because of not wearing the right clothes, going on skiing holidays, etc. This liminal existence intensified when I came out as queer at 17, and further in being diagnosed as dyslexic when I arrived at university. These experiences set the foundation for my values to fight oppression, using the voice which is granted to me from my privileged position as a white person, but also knowing when to clear the space for others to speak so I can learn from them.

Rachel: I qualified as a clinical psychologist seven years ago, specializing in working with psychological trauma, with additional accreditation as a cognitive behavioural therapy (CBT) practitioner and training in eye movement desensitization and reprocessing (EMDR).

My training and experience also include systemic approaches. I am Academic Director, Director of Studies and CBT Accreditation Lead for the University of Bath Doctorate in Clinical Psychology. I provide CBT therapy and supervision and I work clinically in the intensive care units at the Royal United Hospitals, Bath. I have worked in London in research, the voluntary sector, NHS clinical settings and national bodies related to the safety and quality of NHS healthcare. My work in quality improvement, learning from and prevention of patient safety incidents, and planning for and responding to mass-casualty events, fits with my perspective that clinical psychology is critical at the individual, team, organizational, cultural and broadest systemic levels. I believe it has something important to offer in prevention, understanding and responding to consequences.

I am a white middle-class woman who grew up in coastal towns as part of a military family. My upbringing was stable and supported by a wider network of close family. My work in patient safety, quality improvement, military mental health and intensive care have origins in my personal experiences. I was privileged by a good education and postcode access to a selective secondary school that catered well to my needs. A period of family crisis that started during my first year of university flipped this on its head, and I experi-enced a seismic loss of stability, comfort and choice, while working through significant pain and fear that lasted many years. This experience helps me remember that suffering can happen to anyone at any time, often very unexpectedly. I currently enjoy a career I relish and an excellent work-life balance with a loving and supportive family.

CHAPTER 1

History and Context of Clinical Psychology

This chapter will give an overview of some of the history and context of clinical psychology. This is especially relevant in a book about a profession that considers history, context and experiences to be important.

Where clinical psychology began

Clinical psychology is a profession that
has been around for longer than it has
had a name; humans have probably
been helping other humans with their
wellbeing since the dawn of humanity.
The current discipline of clinical psychology does this in a specific way, but
those such as shamans may have taken
on aspects of helping in ways that look
similar. Many physicians and philos-
ophers in history were theorizing on
what the mind is and how it works many hundreds or
thousands of years ago (Reisman 1991). It was not until the
late 19th century when Lightener Witmer opened a psychological clinic in Pennsylvania, United States, that clinical
psychology became established as a profession (Reisman
1991). However, many of the popular theories drawn upon
in modern clinical psychology developed simultaneously
before this, and some of the relevant ideas and underpinnings will be outlined in what follows.

Freud and the birth of psychotherapy

Sigmund Freud was a physician from Vienna who founded
a method of psychotherapy known as psychoanalysis. His
work (and that of his followers) also formed the basis of
psychodynamic psychotherapy. After setting up private

practice and treating people using hypnosis, he soon realized that allowing patients to talk freely (free association) appeared more helpful. This work led to the development of his theory of the unconscious, and dream analysis. Though not the only physician of his time to be practising a form of psychotherapy, he was one of the most influential.

Some of Freud's key ideas included:

- *The subconscious*: This is the idea that much of our understanding of the world, drives and desires are not in our conscious awareness. The iceberg is a good metaphor to explain this: there is much more going on in our minds underneath that which we are consciously aware of.

- *The id, ego and superego*: Freud theorized that personality comprised these three elements. The id is said to be a person's unconscious instinctual drives and desires. The ego is said to be the rational conscious part of the mind and works to meet the needs of the id in a logical  way. The superego is said to be the moral guide, and Freud suggested this was the last part of personality to develop.

- *Psychosexual stages*: In perhaps the most controversial of Freud's theories, he suggested we pass through stages of psychosexual development which include oral stage, anal stage, phallic stage, latent stage and genital stage. Psychological problems are said to occur when the tasks of each stage are not overcome and people can become stuck; for example, people can become orally fixated with eating or smoking later in life if they received too much or too little oral stimulation through feeding.

- *Defence mechanisms*: Freud suggested that to avoid the experience of anxiety, people use unconscious defence strategies to protect them from the feelings of anxiety. They may repress, deny or project unbearable feelings into others. They may displace their feelings felt in an unsafe environment into a safer one, or might regress back in time to feel safer.

Many aspects of Freud's work can be seen within the work of clinical psychologists, and his foundational theories are drawn upon in approaches to practice. Attachment theory (covered elsewhere in the book) is seen as an offspring of psychodynamic theory, and many clinical psychologists will use this to help understand relational dynamics in their clients' lives. Other ideas, such as transference and countertransference are key in the work of psychoanalytic psychotherapists, but many clinical psychologists will lean on these concepts in their work too.

The influence of society on psychology

Our social context has heavily influenced our conceptualization and understanding of distress. The term 'hysteria' is a useful example to illustrate how this has occurred throughout history. The origins of hysteria can be traced back to ancient Egypt where it was thought that a 'wandering womb' was the cause of emotional upset in women; the ancient Greeks then built on this idea, concluding hysteria, or female distress, was caused by a lack of sexual pleasure; the term 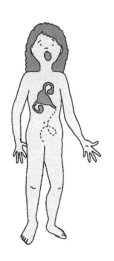 continued to be used to describe female distress, often in a belittling way, with Freud being the first to suggest it could also be a male disorder (Tasca *et al.* 2012). Hysteria was only removed from the *Diagnostic and Statistical Manual of Mental Disorders* (DSM) (covered under later sections in the book, e.g. about the medical model and diagnosis) in 1980, but is still used today in everyday language.

This example demonstrates that societal narratives (in this example, women as irrationally emotional) have a strong influence on the understanding and conceptualization of mental health issues. This is perhaps unsurprising given that we live in a social context where norms shape our understanding of the world. An exploration of the history of clinical psychology is likely to reveal many similar controversial influences on our understanding. Not only has this been problematic, but it has actively fed back into the maintenance of some potentially harmful discourses and power imbalances. Being aware of how history and society have shaped the evolution of clinical psychology allows modern-day clinical psychologists to remain critical about the theories they use in their work.

Structuralism and post-structuralism

Structuralism refers to the school of thought that there are structures and patterns that underpin how the world works. Within this paradigm it is proposed that phenomena such as human experience can be examined and understood within observable and repeatable rules. Humans are therefore assumed to be objectively testable to produce reliable and valid knowledge about the world that can be universally applied. Structuralist ideas evolved alongside the scientific revolution and are now predominant in Western psychology.

Within clinical psychology, structuralist thinking can be seen in the concepts of diagnosis and insight. Diagnostic criteria are determined by others' 'truth' of the world and assume that a combination of set behaviours, thoughts and ways of seeing the world are dysfunctional. Structuralists suggest that people either have or do not have insight into their mental health condition; their level of insight is also defined by others.

Structuralist approaches suggest just one worldview, and post-structuralist approaches question this monochrome view of the world. They question that there is one 'truth' that governs how we should or should not be, think or feel. The differences between structuralist and post-structuralist ways of thinking can be seen in research, by considering the differences between realist approaches in quantitative research, and relativist stances in qualitative research. These terms are discussed in other areas of this book.

Behaviourism

In 1913, John B. Watson was key to behaviourism being established. Purist forms of behaviourism propose that all behaviours are conditioned (learned) through our interactions with the world around us, regardless of other influences such as genetics. Behavioural scientists study what is directly observable and what is measurable. What happens inside a person's 'mind' (thoughts) and 'heart' (emotions) is not focused on by purist behaviourists, who just focus on behaviour. 'Learning theory' is key to behaviourism, where learning is said to happen through 'classical' or 'operant' conditioning.

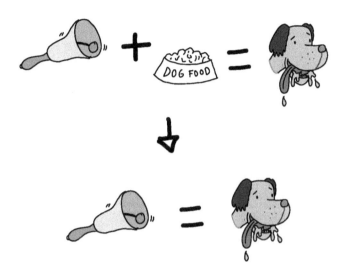

Through classical conditioning, an environmental factor can be 'conditioned' to become the trigger for a physical/ biological response when it is paired repeatedly with something else. Ivan Pavlov showed this by 'conditioning' dogs to link a bell ringing with being fed; eventually they would produce saliva when they heard a bell ringing, even when food was not provided. Through operant conditioning, it is proposed (e.g. by B.F. Skinner) that a behaviour will keep happening if it is reinforced or will 'die out' if it is punished or not reinforced.

Behaviourism is one foundation for behavioural therapies and cognitive behavioural therapies (CBT). Behaviourism informs how mental health difficulties are conceptualized and treated using these approaches.

For example, phobias could be conceptualized as developing through 'classical' conditioning. The physiological fear response could be learned to be triggered by a seemingly safe stimulus, such as a picture of a spider, or the thought of speaking in public; this linking happens over time through interaction with the environment. From a behaviourist perspective, avoidance behaviours reinforce chronic anxiety through 'operant' conditioning; for example, someone who has panic attacks in crowds learns that leaving or avoiding the situation rewards them with a more desirable feeling (absence of anxiety); this then leads to their anxiety growing because the feared situation is never experienced, making it more frightening.

Cognitive psychology

Cognitive psychology developed, in part, as a response to behaviourism and behaviourists' lack of focus on, or interest in, studying and understanding what happened 'in the mind'. Cognitions are considered the internal mental processes for gaining information and understanding using data from the senses, previous experiences and thinking. Cognitive psychologists try to better understand different cognitive processes, such as consciousness, perception, attention, information-processing, problem-solving, language and memory through scientific research. Parallels are often drawn between cognitive psychology and computing. Cognitive psychologists propose that by presenting people with different or changing stimuli (inputs) and then recording the impact (outputs), you can determine what might be happening in the middle (processes of the mind/ brain).

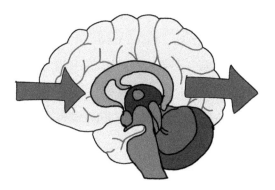

Cognitive psychology is the foundation for understanding and supporting people with the challenges brought about by learning difficulties (such as dyslexia), learning or intellectual disabilities, brain injury and stroke. In addition, this work has fed into a better understanding of cognitive impairments that can show up as part of low mood/depression, anxiety and issues such as post-traumatic stress disorder.

Social psychology

Social psychology considers a person's thoughts, feelings, emotions and behaviours within a social context. This social context not only influences how people behave, but also how people's behaviour is understood. Social psychologists study phenomena such as group behaviour, prejudice and discrimination, stereotypes and attitudes.

Social psychology research first took off after the Second World War as people became interested in why individuals behave as they do in certain situations. Famous experiments include Milgram's (1963) electric shock study and Zimbardo's prison simulation (Haney, Banks and Zimbardo 1973), both of which increased understanding of conformity, authority, aggression and learned helplessness.

Key theories that influence clinical psychology today came from social psychology, including cognitive dissonance (Festinger 1950), social learning theory (Bandura 1976), social identity theory (Tajfel 1970) and attribution theory (Weiner 1986). In today's era of social media and networking platforms, social psychologists research social identity, social influence, prosocial and antisocial behaviours and loneliness.

Attachment theory

Attachment theory relates to a set of ideas concerning relationship behaviour. Originally developed by British psychologists John Bowlby and Mary Ainsworth (Bretherton 1992), the theory suggests our relationship with our primary caregivers influences patterns in our later relationships (attachment style). When a child is born, they are entirely reliant on others to meet their needs and keep them alive. Attachment theory suggests that how their needs are responded to influences their understanding of how others work and what they need to do to get their needs met.

Early theorizing suggested that behaviour patterns could be categorized into secure, anxious, avoidant and disorganized styles and that these were fixed. But it is now more widely accepted that later relationship experiences can influence and help repair negative early experiences. Attachment theory also forms the basis of many therapeutic approaches aimed at repairing the negative impacts of early traumatic attachment experiences. These include schema therapy, psychodynamic psychotherapy and dyadic developmental psychotherapy.

Critics of attachment theory argue that it ignores the influence of peer relationships and the individual's innate traits, and is heavily focused on the role of the mother as a key caregiver. It is also a difficult construct to measure, though some methods of measuring attachment styles do exist. A heavy focus on the quality of carer relationships can also distract from wider contextual factors (e.g. policies such as austerity that may lead to the withdrawal of support services for parents, and place responsibility solely on a caregiver). The theory has also been met with challenges; for example, some feminist critiques suggesting that the theory was developed in Europe and America to push women who had developed work skills during the war back into the home. Critics also argue that it is a narrow model of child-rearing and does not account for diversity in approaches to child-rearing across the globe.

Psychiatry

The term 'psychiatry' emerged in Europe in the early 1800s, describing the work of people who treated 'mental aliena-tion'. Before this, in places like Britain, a large, barbaric and highly profitable trade had developed to keep people locked up indefinitely, with no access to care or treatment. The mental health difficulties of King George III, and the 'med-ical treatment' he received, led to a British parliamentary inquiry into the treatment of mental health in the wider population.

'Therapeutic asylums' were built in large numbers in the 1800s, with psychiatrists using basic physical techniques such as blood-letting, with very little (if any) success, and with many people often getting worse in conditions that today would not be considered healthy nor healing.

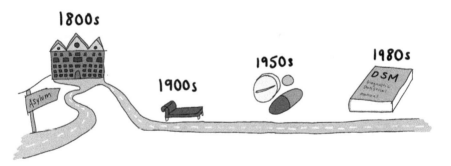

Freud's work in the 1900s triggered a split in how mental ill health was understood and treated; the physical/biological approach vs psychotherapy. Both approaches were provided by psychiatrists but supporting evidence was minimal.

Electro-convulsive (shock) therapies were also developed around this time, and this added to an increasing divide within psychiatry between therapeutic and biological intervention.

In the 1950s and 60s, with the introduction of medications to treat conditions such as psychosis, many patients left asylums and community-based 'outpatient' treatment grew. To create a common language to understand and categorize mental illness, the *Diagnostic and Statistical Manual for Mental Disorders* (DSM) was developed in the 1950s. This allowed for agreed and consistent diagnosis against evidence-based criteria. This led to more effective, and arguably safer, medications; but an understanding of how they work, which patients they work best for, and how the side effects might impact people is still being researched as not enough is yet understood. In addition, who agreed these criteria and who are the participants of this evidence base creates a Western heteronormative bias in understanding mental distress (see section on WEIRD research in Chapter 5).

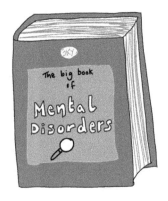

The medical model

The medical model considers mental 'illness' to be understood and treated in the same way as physical illness.

However, critics object to the suggestion that a model that works for the physical body can be transferred to the mind. The medical model lends itself more to psychiatry than psychology, and fits with the concept of diagnosis and the assumption that there is a distinct set of symptoms for all conditions that can be treated medically.

The aspects of physiology that make up the medical model, and are assumed to be related to mental 'illness', are genetics, biochemistry, neuroendocrine factors and neuroanatomy. The medical model has helped with the understanding of some conditions that have an organic cause (e.g. dementia) and when diagnosed, treatment can be quick and cost-effective. For some, the idea of an 'illness' also removes blame and stigma and is considered a benefit of the medical model.

However, critics point out that there is varied evidence about the long-term effectiveness of drug treatments;

little evidence to support the idea of a physical cause for many conditions; side effects of treatment are common; and an 'illness' model for some people can be stigmatizing while not addressing the root cause of their problems (e.g. a toxic living environment). Added to this, diagnoses are not objective (as claimed) and will be influenced by social, cultural and historical factors.

Anti-psychiatry movement

Criticism of inhumane early psychiatry 'treatments' unsurprisingly often came from ex-patients, although very few had the power and/or opportunity to tell their stories. Critique continues in the modern day, but now not just from ex-patients, but  from psychiatrists and psychologists themselves. Psychoanalysts were among those who had proposed that mental illness was not a medical phenomenon, but that societal ills and dysfunctional families shaped an individual's mental wellbeing. They criticized the 'chemical strait jacket' of new psychiatric drugs and pushed to close asylums and provide care in the community (Whitaker 2004).

The emergence of clinical psychology added to this critique, with behaviourists proposing that mental ill health was a learned phenomenon. These different voices came together in the 1960s to form what was referred to as 'the anti-psychiatry movement'. Despite the range of philosophical positions within this movement, there were common pillars which united objectors: the dominance of the medical model; authority based on spurious sources; human problems being mystified; and oppressive and harmful practice.

In response, new 'treatments' such as therapeutic communities emerged. The use of psychosurgery was stopped, electric shock therapies began to decline, and the doses of psychotropic drugs reduced along with their side effects. The last 50 years have seen both psychiatry and the anti-psychiatry movement grow. Other social movements have also paved the way for change in psychiatry, such as the gay rights movement that pushed for the removal of homosexuality as a mental illness. This was only removed from the DSM in 1974 and other sexual orientation disorders in 2013, reflecting the need for us to remain critical and open, given that these changes were within very recent history.

Politics within the profession

Clinical psychology is inherently political. Some might argue that clinical psychologists should focus solely on individualized treatments and the profession be apolitical. However, every person a clinical psychologist works with exists within a social and political context that will influence their mental health. Compton and Shim (2015) have developed a useful model to illustrate this (see figure). Holding the knowledge and power that psychologists do, and doing nothing, could draw criticism of bystanding, or even of complicity in harmful systems that contribute to distress.

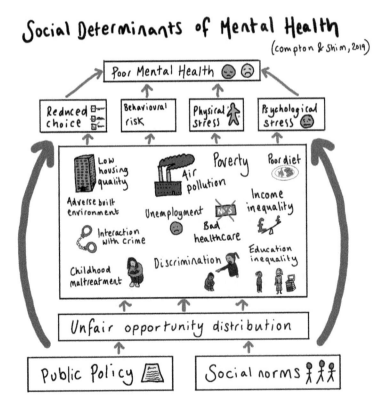

Social Determinants of Mental Health
(Compton & Shim, 2019)

Poverty is an example of how politics is highly relevant to the work of clinical psychologists (Rahim and Cooke 2019). Local and national policies have a direct influence on the social conditions of communities, and when these are restrictive, they can directly negatively affect mental health (McGrath, Walker and Jones 2016). Those with mental health problems are also more likely to live in poverty (Barry and Jenkins 2007), creating a negative reinforcing maintenance cycle of poverty and mental ill health.

Practice guidance is clear on the need for psychologists to consider prevention of mental health issues (British Psychological Society 2019; Department of Health 2019; World Health Organization 2014), therefore they have a role in supporting policy to do this. Key skills that can be helpful in this are: research skills; interpersonal skills for engaging different interested parties; specialist knowledge of the reasons behind distress; and skills for working with systems.

Some psychologists believe that involving themselves in politics is against a key objective of the clinical psychology role to provide therapy. But both can occur: psychologists can deliver good quality therapy *and* influence policy change. We live within a professional ecosystem, and while it is important that some psychologists do focus their energy on developing better therapies, others can use their knowledge, skills and positions to address the conditions that lead to poor mental health in the first place.

Experts by experience

Working collaboratively with people who have personal experience of the difficulties, treatments and services clinical psychologists work with is a core element of the profession. These 'experts by experience' are also known as 'people with personal experience', 'service users', 'clients', 'patients' and 'carers' (not an exhaustive list – there is no clear agreement on the terminology). What is most appropriate or favoured by those the term represents will differ depending on personal preference and the setting in which it is being used. Here we will use 'experts by experience'.

In clinical psychology, experts by experience are people who have direct personal experience of a mental or clinical health problem, learning disability or neurodiversity that means they may, at some point, want, need or benefit from the services provided by a clinical psychologist. The term can also encompass family members, friends and carers.

Experts by experience are essential co-producers in the understanding of mental health issues, their impact and how care and support, assessments and treatment should best be developed and provided. In best practice, they work in truly collaborative partnership in all stages of health awareness and promotion; research; guideline development; advocacy; policy; regulation; and service design, development, provision, evaluation and improvement.

'Experts by experience' and 'experts by education' are not distinct groups, with many overlaps and dual identities existing in the field of clinical psychology: many clinical psychologists will have their own experience of poor mental health or use mental health services.

Individualism, collectivism, colonialism and clinical psychology

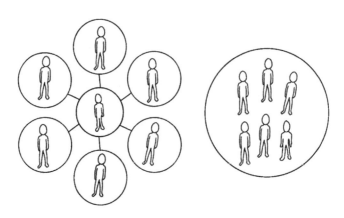

Individualism and collectivism are two ends of a scale of attitudes towards the social world. The values that underpin individualism tend to be about personal growth, meritocracy and self-sufficiency. Values of collectivism connect to community growth, collaboration and sharing. Individualism and collectivism are relevant ideas to clinical psychology because they provide frames on which much clinical psychology work can be hung.

Within clinical psychology, individualistic approaches can be understood as those that place an emphasis on the individual's need to change. This is the primary focus across a multitude of psychotherapeutic approaches where autonomy, self-efficacy and resilience are celebrated. It is also the

approach focused on by most clinical psychologist training courses, with few looking at community-level engagement and more collectivist ways of working. Individualism aligns strongly with the Western capitalist and neoliberal focus on 'every person for themselves'.

More collectivist cultures might consider healing as a communal responsibility. Individuals are seen as inextricably part of those around them and therefore community wellbeing is integral to an individual's wellbeing. This view considers improving mental health as everyone's responsibility and shifts the emphasis from individual interventions, though does not obstruct them. Clinical psychologists can facilitate individual therapy while aligning with and respecting collectivism. However, it is important for clinical psychologists to remain critical and reflexive in clinical work to consider that individual therapy may not be the right thing for someone, and a community intervention may be more suitable.

Because most theories, models and interventions in clinical psychology focus on the internal world of the individual (thoughts-emotions-behaviour), this Western perspective is thought of as colonizing how mental distress is understood. Some suggest that this makes it a 'white Western psychology for white Western people' and potentially pathologizes those outside of this (Wood and Patel 2017). Indeed, aspects of clinical psychology have an upsetting and disturbing history, linked to regimens that have actively oppressed and tormented people that do not fit these norms; for example, apartheid (systemic/policy-driven segregation and discrimination on the basis of 'race') (Padmanabhanunni *et al.* 2022) or eugenics (controlling who could have children to enhance heritable attributes that were deemed to be 'desirable') (Yanos 2018).

Outside of the West, cultures that focus on family, community, culture and nature (Ciofalo 2019), celebrate spirituality, something that has less space in scientist-practitioner Western models of psychology. The very practice of 'science' or research is shaped by cultural context. In the West, there is an emphasis on objectivity, expertise, observation and reporting. Whereas non-Western psychologies may focus instead on critical consciousness and praxis (action and reflection) (Freire 1970), building relationships in order to give back to communities and co-producing research with a focus on interdependence rather than positioning psychologists as objective detached experts.

Clinical psychology training courses are beginning to work on decolonization in naming and critiquing this Western frame. But it is just the start of the journey and there is much work to be done to ensure this work is not tokenistic and leads to real change.

CHAPTER 2

Who Are Clinical Psychologists and Where Do They Work?

This chapter will give an overview of some of the attributes of clinical psychologists. Which of these are considered most important is likely to vary between people, but we hope to give an overview. We will also talk about how people come into the profession, where they may work and what they may do day to day.

Attributes of a clinical psychologist

Because of the variety of work a clinical psychologist can become involved in, they must be able to draw on a wide range of attributes. A clinical psychologist is expected to continually review, build, refine and nurture the attributes that are necessary to meet the demands of their roles. This includes personal and professional attributes, which sometimes overlap.

A person's natural disposition, moral compass, values, background, training, theoretical beliefs, stance on what the role of a clinical psychologist is, personal and professional experiences and their current context will all have an impact on what they 'bring' to their roles and identity as a clinical psychologist. You could think of a clinical psychologist as having a stock of different ingredients and utensils that they add more or less of at different times for different needs and intended outcomes.

Clinical psychologists will differ on what they see as key attributes to develop, maintain and reflect on during their career. The examples below give an idea of those that may be important:

- empathy and compassion (not to be confused with sympathy)
- self-awareness, self-care and self-regulation
- reflexivity
- setting and maintaining personal and professional boundaries
- active listening and clear communication
- trustworthiness
- curiosity and openness
- tolerating distress and uncertainty
- exploring different perspectives, or the background to different views
- theorizing, formulating, conceptualizing and hypothesizing
- identifying, understanding and making sense of data and patterns
- testing things out and experimenting
- applying theory and research to real-world problems (e.g. through provision of therapy)
- developing and sharing knowledge (e.g. through research)
- nurturing and developing others and themselves (e.g. through reflective practice, supervision and training)
- connecting and working with others
- advocating, standing alongside and making space for others
- leadership
- management
- balancing lots of different demands and priorities at once

- development of tools, techniques, processes and services
- changing perspectives, narratives and systems.

Clinical psychology career journeys

In the UK, to qualify as a clinical psychologist you must complete a professional doctorate in clinical psychology, which is accredited by the professional bodies. The courses are often co-hosted by universities and the NHS. In order to practise as a clinical psychologist in the UK, and use the protected title of 'Practitioner Psychologist', you must register with the Health and Care Professions Council (HCPC).

Individuals enter clinical psychology training in the UK with a diverse range of experiences, but it is highly competitive to get onto a course. Currently, applications are managed through the Clearing House for Postgraduate Courses in Clinical Psychology, which gives information about the different programmes, how to apply and criteria to get on.

Courses have some similar components due to standardization of training by the commissioning, accrediting and regulating bodies, although there are also large variations, reflecting different influences and values. Trainees specialize in research and latter placements during their courses and their career paths will diverge further after training.

One clinical psychologist will have a very different looking journey to another, one example is illustrated here:

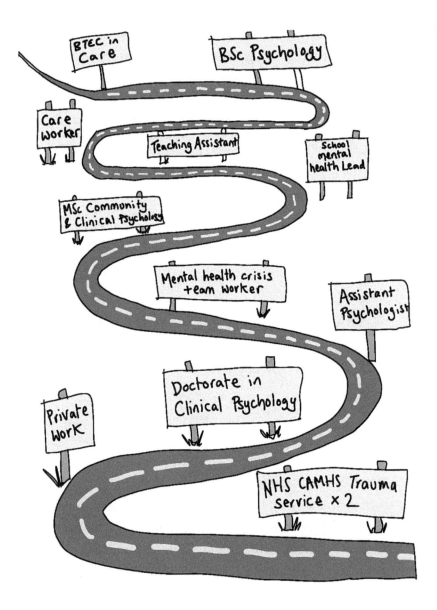

Examples of the settings where clinical psychologists work

Clinical psychologists work in a wide variety of settings; the types of settings and roles within them are so broad that the examples in this section are far from exhaustive. However, we hope to give a sense of the variety.

Secondary-care mental health services for adults

The 'secondary-care' element refers to it being the next step along from the front-line mental health support that people get from primary-care services such as a general practitioner (GP) appointment. The needs of the people being assessed and supported in secondary-care services are often more complex, long-standing and proving more difficult to change. In these services in the UK, a clinical psychologist may be responsible for providing psychological advice, consultation, training and supervision to other members of the care team; assessments and conceptualizations (formulations) of the problems someone is experiencing; individual or group therapy; and often some form of management or leadership role. They may develop a specialism within the team but are usually expected to be able to work with people presenting with a wide variety of difficulties.

Child and adolescent mental health services (CAMHS)

CAMHS exist to serve the mental health needs of children and young people. In the UK, CAMHS teams generally exist in most areas and include generic and more specialized services. Generic CAMHS services are ever evolving and often under pressure from long waiting lists. Children are typically referred in by a professional

because there is a concern for their mental health. Many CAMHS services then assess the child's mental health needs and provide individualized or family-based interventions. Professionals may also liaise with other agencies and work with the systems around children. When it comes to prevention, work is sometimes put into secondary prevention (preventing the escalation of mental health difficulties), but it is not typical for CAMHS to conduct primary prevention interventions (intervening with the conditions that lead to poor mental health in the first place).

Older adults

Working as a clinical psychologist with older adults can be complex and rewarding. Older people often have intersecting physical issues (e.g. mobility or sensory decline, use of medication), psychological factors (e.g. loneliness, loss, isolation) and sociocultural factors (e.g. lack of socially valued roles, lack of social and community support, financial stresses), and these are on top of what one might ordinarily expect to see in a psychology service (anxiety, depression, bipolar disorder, etc.). As well as in wider society, older people also face discrimination in mental health services, with adults over 65 not having the same access to specialist mental health services as those under 65 (Royal College of Psychiatrists 2009). This is due both to individual factors. such as potential cohort effects (e.g. 'stiff upper lip' mentality, commonly associated with previous generations, and stigma around mental health problems), and to service factors (differences in presentation mean physical health might be prioritized over emotional distress).

A clinical psychologist working with older adults will be considering these intersectional issues alongside therapeutic work. There also may be more systemic work needs where an older adult relies more on, and is therefore more heavily influenced by, the family and support network context.

Learning disability (LD) services

Learning disability services (sometimes known as intellectual disability services) work with people who have diagnosed and suspected mild to severe learning disabilities, as well as with their families, carers and other support services in a more systemic way. Interventions may include direct therapy, systemic therapy, team

formulation, and positive behaviour support. People with learning disabilities tend to face multiple disadvantages and are highly vulnerable to abuse and maltreatment, and therefore mental health issues may develop from traumatizing and disempowering experiences. They are more likely to have barriers in communication, and there is an increasing focus on participation and service user voice in learning disability services.

Physical health teams and hospitals

Clinical psychologists will often work in hospitals and health teams in cancer, cardiac, respiratory, renal, head injury, stroke, pain, sexual health, chronic fatigue and diabetes teams. They might focus on: supporting people adjusting to diagnoses or to changes in how they look from surgery, hair loss and scarring; helping them improve how they are able to engage with their healthcare, medication and rehabilitation; reducing barriers to successful communication between healthcare staff and patients; supporting patients to have difficult conversations with their friends and families; and planning for end-of-life care with dignity and choice. As an example of what a clinical psychologist in this setting may do, in intensive care units (ICUs) they can provide bedside psychological assessments and interventions to patients on the unit; deliver support

and guidance to families, and give advice, consultation, training and psychological support to the staff.

Neuropsychology

To work as a neuropsychologist requires the completion of either a paediatric or adult master's in neuropsychology after completing clinical, educational or counselling psychology training. However, many clinical psychologists  also offer neuropsychology services as part of their role (e.g. testing for cognitive decline in a memory clinic with older adults). As well as offering psychometric testing to assess cognitive strengths and weaknesses and offer advice and strategies to compensate for difficulties, clinical psychologists might work with the individual, partner or family impacted by cognitive change (e.g. following a stroke) to manage the emotional impact, any challenging behaviour, adjustment to life changes or provide education about why these changes have happened.

Forensic settings

Alongside forensic psychologists, clinical psychologists also work in forensic settings (prison, secure hospitals, rehabilitation). Clinical psychologists in these settings provides assessments and formulations to help understand why people have committed crimes and how these are impacted by and impact on their mental health. These formulations lead to interventions to help people avoid committing crimes in future, as well as deal with the mental health difficulties. The work includes motivating and engaging people in doing psychological work, with a focus on creating internal stability and behavioural change (e.g. anger management programmes); they may also be involved in a programme to address specific offences (e.g. sexual offending). The assessment of risk is also a critical part of the role, both to others and to oneself, and this may include neuropsychology testing. Clinical psychologists will also help people prepare for transition once their sentence is coming to an end, including helping the changes the person has made to remain embedded.

Team working

Clinical psychologists are commonly part of a team or service made up of many different types of professionals that provide different functions. Clinical psychologists tend to provide a wide range of services in a team and take on leadership responsibility for aspects of work. Clinically, for example, they might provide neuropsychology tests, reports and diagnoses for individual patients; specialist psychological assessment and therapy for particular presenting difficulties such as psychosis; family therapy clinics; or run group interventions to address issues like anxiety, anger, problem drinking or low mood.

Clinical psychologists will use their training, experience and expertise in understanding systems; empathic listening; critically reviewing literature and guidelines; quantitative and qualitative data collection, analysis and reporting; assessment, formulation and case conceptualization; individual and group interventions; and teaching, supervision, leadership and management to help teams design, develop, deliver, review, evaluate and learn from good practice.

Working with complexity

Clinical psychologists tend to work with complexity in all aspects of their work. Training provides opportunity to develop skills for assimilating multiple strands of information and difficulties and applying these to improve people's lives. Complexity might be because of the intersection of mental and physical health, of someone's living environment and lifestyle, the severity and longevity of their symptoms, suicidal ideation and/or trauma (Ruscio and Holohan 2006). Clinical psychologists have a range of models, methods and techniques that can be deployed flexibly to work with complex issues. These can be applied on an individual, family or systems level (e.g. a care home, NHS organization or distinct group within society).

Working with complexity is a skill that can be transferred to other elements of a clinical psychologist's role. The service structures we work in can be multi-layered and complex, and people often sit between multiple services. Holding complexity is also a big element of risk management.

A 'day in the life' of a clinical psychologist

Clinical psychologists have highly varied job responsibilities, with one day rarely looking the same as another. Below are examples from two of the authors' working days to give a flavour of the variety of clinical psychology practice.

Working across a clinical health role in the NHS and a training role in a university:

9:00–10:00	Clinical supervision for a trainee clinical psychologist
10:00–12:00	Time spent in the intensive care unit with four different patients assessing psychological issues, risk assessing and offering guidance and advice to the individual, families and nursing staff
12:00–12:30	Clinical notes and emails
12:30–13:30	Lunch and drive to university for second role
13:30–14:30	Research supervision meeting with student
15:00–16:00	Marking a case study from a trainee clinical psychologist
16:00–17:00	Lecture to master's students

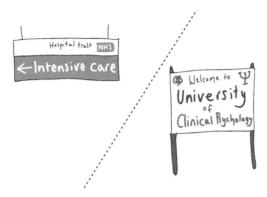

Working in a trauma-focused CAMHS for young asylum seekers:

8:00–9:00	Network meeting with professionals working with asylum seekers living in hotels
9:00–10:15	Weekly service planning meeting with the service lead
10:15–10:30	Tea break and a check-in with the assistant psychologists in the office
10:30–12:00	Initial assessment with young person, family and interpreters
12:00–12:30	Lunch
12:30–13:30	Supervision with the assistant psychologist
13:30–14:00	Emails and preparation for group
14:00–16:00	Psychoeducation group with six male teenagers who speak three languages between them
16:00–17:00	Debrief with the assistant psychologist, emails and record keeping

Leadership

Leadership is a key skill of clinical psychologists, and many hold leadership and management roles. Leadership is different from management. The latter is concerned with maintaining organizational functioning and how individuals are contributing to that. Leadership is more concerned with direction setting and inspiring individuals to contribute to a functional system. Many training courses teach systemic skills, and this knowledge and way of thinking is directly transferable to leadership of organizations and systems. Many of the people skills needed in leadership parallel those used by clinical psychologists in therapy.

Clinical psychologists are often leaders in service functioning. They possess key skills for engaging with and empowering people to make decisions that are functional in a compassionate way that can lead to meaningful change. Within services, they may be supervisors and lead on aspects of service function and operation.

The key skills in research and evaluation that come with the scientist-practitioner role are highly useful in service development. Clinical psychologists have the research skills to evaluate what is happening, systems-based skills to think about complexity and people, and organizational skills to implement change.

It is important to note that leadership is not about a hierarchical system and your position within it. It is an attribute that can be developed, and those early in their clinical psychology journeys may demonstrate leadership skills in: how they support, advocate for or mentor others; how they promote a cause important to them; and how they suggest ideas or creative solutions to problems.

CHAPTER 3

Key Clinical Psychologist Skills and Tools

Clinical psychologists possess a range of skills and are trained to draw on different approaches in their work. These skills often become more specialized (or change direction) as someone moves through their career and some psychologists will predominantly draw on one therapy modality.

Other psychologists may work less with individuals and more with teams and wider systems.

This chapter introduces what assessment can look like, what formulation is and how intervention differs across different ways of working. There will be an introduction to key ideas and ways of working, with a whistle-stop tour of different therapeutic approaches.

Supervision

The word 'supervision' derives from the Latin words *super* (above) and *videre* (to observe, or provide oversight). Supervision is typically a space to review clinical work, and support development. It is a process that is embedded in the work of aspirating and practising clinical psychologists and outlined as an expectation in professional practice guidelines. Supervision can be provided on a one-to-one basis or to a group of supervisees.

Supervision usually takes place as a scheduled meeting, where the supervisor and supervisee will agree an agenda and work through the items they have each brought to the session. Supervision time should be protected and prioritized by both parties as an essential element of clinical psychology work. This is likely to be one hour per month for those with experience, but often much more frequent for trainee, assistant and newly qualified clinical psychologists. Contracting at the start of a supervisory relationship is important to ensure joint expectations of how it will work and be most useful. When training, supervisors may sit in and observe the supervisee's work or watch recordings made with the client's consent. This supports the supervisee and supervisor to reflect on the work, build skills and tackle challenges together.

Supervision is intended to be supportive and developmental and to offer a safe space. Unfortunately, this is not always the case, and some people can experience very challenging supervision contexts. Having different supervisors for line management, clinical supervision and professional practice is a way to mitigate the impact of difficult supervision relationships where possible.

Power is inherently present in the supervision space, thus failure to attend to power dynamics in supervision can have negative consequences. It is the responsibility of both the supervisor and supervisee to attend to the issues of power, and the impact of this on the function and safety of the supervision relationship.

Therapeutic relationship

The quality of the relationship between a therapist and the person they are working with is understood to be one of the most important influences on the outcome of therapy (Horvath *et al.* 2011; Martin, Garske and Davis 2000). This is regardless of the type of therapy being used. Clinical psychologists will often see the therapeutic relationship as a foundation on which their work sits.

Carl Rogers (1965), an American psychologist who pioneered person-centred psychotherapy, suggested there are three key attitudes of a therapist:

Therapeutic Relationship

- congruence or genuineness in the relationship
- unconditional positive regard and acceptance
- empathy and congruence.

Clinical psychologists will usually be highly skilled in attuning to people's interpersonal feedback and adapting their approach accordingly, and this is likely to create an environment where trust can develop. Having a good therapeutic relationship is not just important at the beginning of work, but throughout so that the challenges therapy brings can be withstood. Sometimes the clinical psychologist will get it wrong and the therapeutic relationship can be ruptured. But the hope is it will be collaboratively repaired again, a process which in itself can be therapeutic and lead to a deeper sense of trust over time.

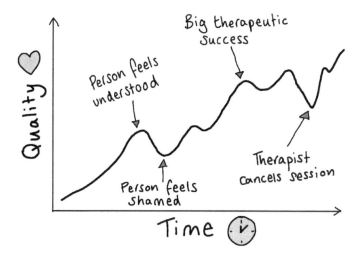

Many clinical psychologists will draw on elements of attachment theory when considering the therapeutic alliance and what people might bring into the therapy room (more on attachment theory in Chapter 1); to some degree a clinical psychologist is in both a position of authority and nurture – dynamics which replicate the role of an attachment figure. This then activates what is known as an internal working model (IWM), the way in which someone has learned to see themselves, others and the world. The IWM is like a lens through which the relationship is viewed, which ultimately influences how that individual responds within the therapeutic relationship.

It is important for clinical psychologists to reflect on

power and how they might be viewed and experienced within the therapeutic relationship. No matter how warm and collaborative a clinical psychologist is, they are in a position of power. People may have had negative experiences of those in authority previously, and this could amplify the power imbalance and will affect how the clinical psychologist is perceived. These dynamics could be reflected on explicitly or within supervision to ensure they are being attended to.

The scientist-practitioner model

The scientist-practitioner model is thought to have first been publicly promoted in 1949 in Colorado at the Conference on Graduate Education in Psychology. As with most things in clinical psychology, it has evolved over time but remains a core value of clinical psychology training and practice. Shapiro (1967) referred to clinical psychology as an applied science, and there was a notion that clinical psychologists had a responsibility to ensure money (e.g. public funding in the UK's NHS) was spent appropriately on effective and efficient practice derived from knowledge not simply conjecture.

The scientist-practitioner model called for clinical psychologists to be trained both as psychological practitioners and scientists. As the model developed, the importance of the reciprocal relationship between the practitioner and scientist aspects was strengthened so that the two areas were then taught together, not separately. Their interdependencies and influences on each other were seen to be as important to understand and master as the separate areas.

As a scientist-practitioner, a clinical psychologist is expected to apply what is 'known' to psychological assessment and interventions through an understanding of the evidence base, existing literature and gaps/unknowns. They are also expected to apply their scientist skills of theory/hypothesis generation; observation, measurement and data gathering, and testing things out.

Clinical practice and research inform and update each other. The model suggests this not only supports the most appropriate methods of assessment and intervention to be used but ensures the whole field of clinical psychology keeps evolving to meet new challenges and environments and to make use of new scientific understanding and technology. The clinical psychologist is a receiver, interpreter, tester and generator of knowledge.

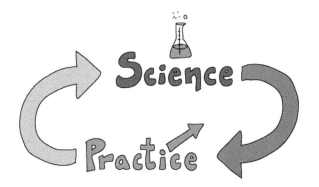

Reflexive-scientist-practitioner model

Since the 1980s, the term reflexive-practitioner has been used as an alternative model to the scientist-practitioner. This model emphasizes the importance of clinical psychologists being self-aware and considers how the clinical psychologist as a person impacts on the therapeutic experience, as well as being impacted upon by it. Clinical psychologists are therefore required to consider their own assumptions and where these might have come from, as well as other influences such as their racialized identity or gender. Clinical psychologists must practise under supervision and can explore this self-reflexivity within the supervisory relationship.

Reflection is a mental process inherent in being human, relating to careful thought and a way of learning from experience. Reflective practice and reflexivity (reflecting back on oneself and one's own actions) is central to the education, development and practice of healthcare professionals, including clinical psychologists. Being a reflexive practitioner requires a clinical psychologist to be aware of their own biases, and how these might impact on their work in helpful

or harmful ways. In addition, the evidence base drawn on in the scientist-practitioner model has holes (see Chapter 5) as some populations are not represented within it. One way to respond to this in the absence of appropriate evidence, is for clinical psychologists to draw on their reflective and reflexive practice to collaborate with clients to adapt an intervention that fits with their lived experience of the world.

Clinical psychologists are expected to develop reflexivity and reflective practice skills, and support others to do so too. By providing dedicated time for reflective practice, clinical psychologists actively work to develop a reflective state of mind and make sense of things that have happened in their practice. They might do this on their own, with others who have shared an experience, in supervision or in reflective practice groups.

Two key models of reflective practice and learning through reflection are Kolb's Learning Cycle (Kolb 2014) and Gibbs' Reflective Cycle (Gibbs 1988). Using the Gibbs Reflective Cycle, the reflective practitioner starts with describing what happened in detail, moving on to feelings about what happened, then on to making evaluations about what was good and what was bad about the situation. The next step is analysis about how this could be made sense of (e.g. drawing on theories, research or available literature). Conclusions are then drawn (e.g. what else could have been done), and this leads on to an action plan should a similar situation arise in the future.

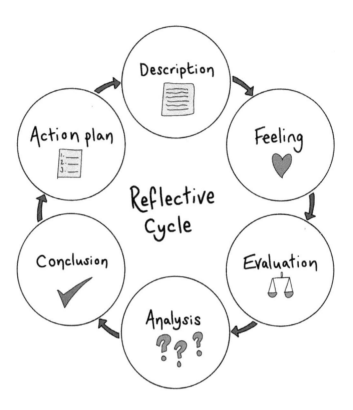

The British Psychological Society states that reflective practice and reflexivity can support the clinical psychologist's self-care and wellbeing, as well as psychologically informed practice (BPS 2017). It is well known that professionals' improved wellbeing and self-care are related to better and safer healthcare, so reflective practice is good both for clinical psychologists and for the people they work with.

The reflexive-scientist-practitioner is an amalgamation of the scientist-practitioner and reflexive-practitioner models, perhaps to get the best of both worlds. So, a clinical psychologist should aim to be aware of how they influence and interpret practice and research. They should recognize that their subjectivity can limit and shape their knowledge and understanding.

Assessment overview

One of the first tasks of clinical psychologists when they start working with people or groups is to carry out an assessment. Assessment is essentially gathering lots of pieces of a puzzle so that an understanding of the difficulties can start to be formed. This assessment often provides the underlying understanding on which intervention may sit. Assessments can be completed quickly, but many clinical psychologists will see assessment as an ongoing process.

There will be similarities across all assessments, like what the main difficulties are or what needs to change. But the assessment information being sought will differ depending on the theoretical model and service function. For example, in a secondary mental health service where CBT is the main intervention modality, questions about history may be asked, but there will be more of a focus on current thoughts, feelings and behaviours. Conversely, in a service for care-experienced children, details of early experiences and attachment behaviours would be privileged. Questions about the system around a person may be asked in all assessments because clinical psychologists tend to hold in mind the system influence to different degrees across all modalities. Though, in more systemic assessments, questions will be asked about relationship patterns, roles and wider system pressures.

Though they can be more targeted, clinical psychology assessments are not usually prescriptive. The psychologist will be asking questions based on responses to other questions and information. Assessment is a bit like peeling back layers of an onion, where clinical psychologists will be asking questions based on the responses to questions that came before. The process of assessment requires initiative, reflexivity and knowledge, all things that can be developed over time.

As professionals with a duty of care to those they are working with, clinical psychologists will often need to assess risk alongside other assessment questions. This requires them to draw on interpersonal skills so that difficult questions can be asked in a way that enables the person to feel as comfortable as possible when sharing what can be very sensitive and potentially shame-inducing information.

Assessment is never entirely complete, because eliciting more information about a psychological difficulty or person's context will continue after an initial assessment. Assessment is happening in parallel to the development of trust and the person's own understanding of their difficulty. This means that more information may come forward as a therapeutic relationship develops more perceived safety. But there will need to be enough information gathered to start to form a picture of what has happened and what is going on, and to be able to move towards a formulation/ theory about what might help.

Assessment and management of risk

Assessing and managing risk is a core element of a clinical psychologist's role. How risk is understood and defined is likely to vary across settings, but is often about risk of harm coming to a person the clinical psychologist is working with. The risk may be linked to the likelihood of self-harm, a person ending their life, risk of poor long-term outcomes, or other potential scenarios. Risk might also be at a group level or be more systemic in nature (e.g. organizational, cultural or global, such as conflict, terror and pandemics). As well as managing risk of harm in clinical settings, risk assessment and management applies in research and leadership roles.

A risk assessment can never fully predict the future,

but will offer a structured reflection on the potential of an outcome occurring. This allows decisions to be made about whether there is a need to respond to risks and, if so, to what degree. When assessing the risk of someone coming to harm, the process should be collaborative and rely on: knowledge of any relevant research evidence combined with knowledge of the individual patient/group/service/ setting and the wider context (e.g. social support network for patients); knowledge of previous events; the perspectives of all those people involved; and clinical/professional judgement. Good risk assessments will also identify 'protective factors' – things seen to reduce the risk of negative outcomes. A risk assessment can lead to a risk management or crisis plan for individuals or organizations.

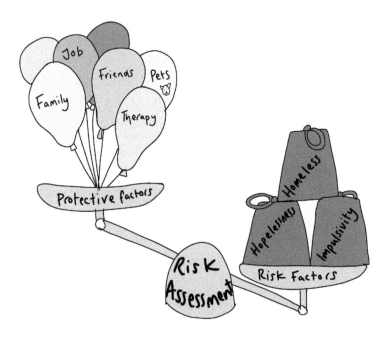

Risk assessment can sometimes be simplified to a red, amber, green system which loses more nuanced and descriptive ways of understanding and communicating risk. Best practice in risk assessment and management now recognizes that risk decisions, plans and communications should be made based on a variety of information and offer more detail than this. Clinical psychologists use their skills and knowledge of psychology to assimilate information to undertake risk assessment. It may also be important to support professionals to 'hold' the uncertainty that harm will occur, and that working to prevent every risk of harm may actually be detrimental to someone.

Some clinical psychologists will use structured risk assessment tools to assess the risk of harm to an individual or those around them (e.g. within forensic services). These can influence aspects of someone's care or restrictions on liberty and so have to be done by specialists who understand the tools well.

Risk Assessment

Concern:

What makes it worse:

Protective factors:

Action:

Formulation

Formulation is a key skill of clinical psychologists and can be used with individuals, families, teams or wider systems. The term 'formulation' is used to describe the shared understanding or conceptualization of a psychological difficulty.

A formulation is not a diagnosis, nor is it a set explanation of what is wrong, but a starting point that often goes on to inform an intervention. It brings together information elicited during an initial assessment and other sources such as referral information.

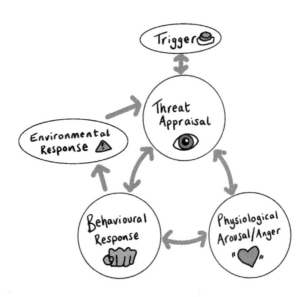

Formulation doesn't have to be about what is 'wrong', and critics of the diagnostic model ask us to reflect on this kind of terminology that locates a problem in an individual rather than their context. A formulation often draws on psychological theory, evidence from  practice, understanding about social context, information gathered during assessment and knowledge from those involved in the process.

Formulations are not fixed and are usually 'best guesses' as to what is going on at a certain point in time with the information that has been gathered so far. Because formulation influences the intervention the psychologist uses, and intervention usually reveals more information about the nature of the problem, the formulation often needs to be updated or refined. Therefore, formulation is an iterative and evolving process which reflects the complexity of human beings and their psychological lives.

Formulation can often be specific to a particular diagnostic or therapeutic model, however, there are some key transdiagnostic, cross-cutting formulation models that have been developed. These are often drawn upon by clinical psychologists when formulating. It is important to note  that it is not just clinical psychologists who use formulation and many other mental health professionals will draw on these approaches in their work.

Five Ps model

A well-known model used to assist clinical psychologists to develop formulation is known as the 'Five Ps' model. Developed by Craig Macniel and colleagues (2012), the model offers a framework for information that can help develop an understanding of someone's difficulties. The five Ps are:

- Presenting problem: What is the difficulty to be understood and changed?
- Predisposing factors: What made someone vulnerable to the difficulty?
- Precipitating factors: What triggered the difficulties?
- Perpetuating factors: What is adding to or keeping the difficulty going?
- Protective factors: What strengths exist to protect against the difficulty?

The model is often used in individual work, but also when psychologists are working with teams.

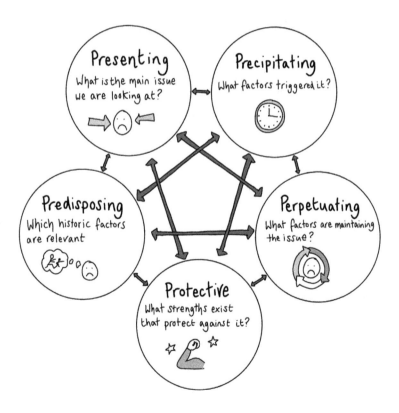

Power Threat Meaning Framework

The Power Threat Meaning Framework (PTMF) is the work of a group of psychologists and people who have used mental health services (Johnstone and Boyle 2018). The group created the framework in response to a critique of the diagnostic model and wanted to develop an alternative tool to understand distress. It aims to understand psychological difficulty as something that arises in a context and is associated with the saying:

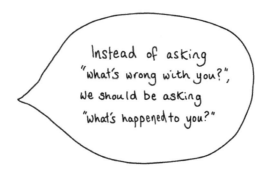

The framework aims to explore experiences of powerlessness, how these affect people, what meaning is taken from them and what people do to cope. This is knitted together in a narrative explanation and is guided by the following questions:

- What happened to you?
- How did this affect you?
- What sense did you make of this?
- What did you do to survive?

The PTMF emphasis on difficulties and dysfunction, being an understandable response to oppressive circumstances, is assumed to reduce shame. When considering structuralist and post-structuralist frameworks (discussed in Chapter 1), the PTMF aligns more with the latter. Clinical psychologists may find the PTFM useful when considering distress for those who are marginalized by society and/or those who have experienced abuse. This is because it considers the context and views what we construct as mental illness as a response to this.

Since its development, critics have suggested that there is a limited evidence base for the PTMF. Some have said this criticism is a moot point, as it is not designed to be a 'treatment' that can be measured. The original document that discussed the PTMF is also very long. However, the

PTMF provides a tool that may be a useful method to collaboratively formulate difficulties, and evaluation of the framework will offer more insight into its usefulness as a model. It can also be applied across teams and communities to help people think about power and responses to this.

Bronfenbrenner's ecological systems theory

Another model that clinical psychologists will often draw on to help consider context when developing formulations is Bronfenbrenner's (1979) ecological systems theory. Though originally developed to think about the systems a child develops within, the model is a useful tool to think about the contextual influences on anyone's life. The model proposes that there are multiple systems that affect our lives. Though clinical psychologists often work directly with an individual or the microsystem around them, some will work to affect change at wider system levels:

- *The microsystem*: The is the closest system of influence on someone's life and may include family, or a place the person attends regularly like work, school or a religious institution. Clinical psychologists may work with the microsystem to support individual work or may solely work with the microsystem. This is often more likely in services working with those with learning disabilities or with children.
- *The mesosystem*: The mesosystem is the interactions between different microsystems. A clinical

psychologist may work to support positive relationships between different people in the microsystem. An example of this may be working to strengthen communication pathways between a school and foster carer.

- *The exosystem*: The exosystem includes things that have a second-hand influence on people's lives. In the context of mental health, this may be the types of mental health services that are commissioned in particular areas or how much green space is available. A clinical psychologist can influence this system by sharing views on media platforms or advising commissioning boards on what is a good use of public health spending.

- *The macrosystem*: The macrosystem is the wider system around people and includes narratives around communities and identities, the economic context of a society or the culture that is heavily embedded in life. A clinical psychologist may influence this by sitting on panels that inform government policy or by contributing to the evidence base that it leans on.

- *The chronosystem*: This refers to changes over time that affect people's lives. For example, changes in women going out to work more may have an impact on how younger women judge their abilities and see possibilities for themselves for their own future ambitions. Clinical psychologists can affect this system by using their power to contribute to research that feeds into changes in policy.

The model is often used within community psychology but can be useful to draw upon in conjunction with different therapy modalities and formulation methods. It can be used as a framework to communicate why intervention on different levels can be important to an individual or community's mental health. Clinical psychologists may find it an accessible tool to think about why someone may not be responding to intervention at an individual level and what needs to change in the wider system to lead to improved wellbeing.

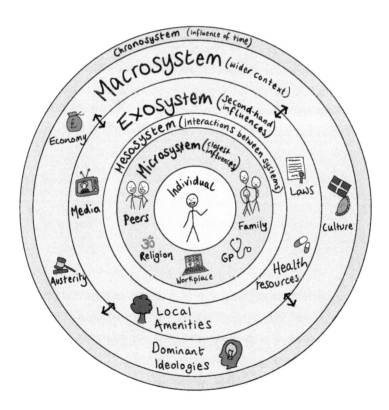

Formulating with families, teams or organizations

Formulation is not always a task for a clinical psychologist to complete with an individual. It can be used with families to think about how patterns are maintaining difficulties. It can also be used with teams to develop a shared understanding of the difficulties someone in the team is working with.

Team formulation can help a team to get in touch with psychological thinking, supporting empathy and the therapeutic benefits of this for all involved. For teams who are under a lot of pressure, it can be useful for clinical psychologists to offer a space to stop and reflect on difficulties for an individual, how this impacts the team and how feedback loops can maintain challenging dynamics. Psychologists may draw on different models depending on the context of the team.

Clinical psychologists will often be working in multidisciplinary teams, and their skills of formulation can be used to think more widely too. They may formulate how systems and services are operating and the dynamics or challenges that maintain problems within and between them.

Flexibility and creativity

Clinical psychology training often provides a whistle-stop tour through a range of models and therapy types and can leave some newly qualified psychologists feeling like a 'Jack (or Jill) of all trades and master of none'. Some courses are more dominated by particular theoretical models and types of therapy, and might also offer standalone qualifications alongside the doctorate qualification.

Some clinical psychologists will be more 'purist' and aligned to specific theoretical models and approaches, whereas others will be more integrative in their work. Integrative could be at the theoretical level, or more like a cook using their knowledge to combine tools and ideas from a multitude of approaches. This ability is sometimes seen as a 'clinical art', where theory, knowledge and methods are applied flexibly and in response to need. Being able to do this confidently in a skilled way, takes experience, training and support through the supervisory relationship. Reflexivity is important in this, where the clinical psychologist will be reflecting on how they are working with someone and taking on feedback to adapt their style and approach accordingly.

Diagnosis and the medical model

Clinical psychologists tend to use formulation rather than diagnose mental health illnesses. However, some will diagnose or suggest symptoms that are in line with diagnostic criteria. Diagnosis is heavily embedded in the systems that clinical psychologists work in, and it can also be a shared language between professionals, people who have been given a diagnosis and families. In some parts of the world, diagnosis is what is needed to access health insurance to obtain any mental health support. Diagnosis is used in research as a way of understanding what treatments will work for whom and in what contexts, and it can also be a shared language for professionals planning interventions. For those receiving a diagnosis, it can be a mixed experience. Some people find it a validating way to explain their current experiences or to access more support. For others, diagnosis can feel dehumanizing, and leading to assumptions and negative treatment from others.

The *Diagnostic and Statistical Manual of Mental Disorders* (DSM) (American Psychiatric Association 2013) or the *International Classification of Diseases* (ICD) (World Health Organization 2019) are the main guides for diagnosis. Both of these classification tools are updated periodically, in line with research and new understandings; DSM is now DSM-5 and ICD is now ICD-11. Sometimes they differ in how they classify mental illnesses; this means that a person may get a diagnosis using one manual but not the other. Consequently, it can get very confusing in clinical practice and research.

For diagnosis, information is collected from a range of sources, in a range of ways, including standardized assessment tools. Data gathered will most likely include the impact of difficulties on a person's life ('impact on functioning') and how long problems have been persisting for. They will use these data to identify whether a diagnosis fits and, very importantly, to make sense of the issues a person is bringing to them (the

'presenting problem'). Some diagnoses require exclusion of other options for them to be given, (e.g. for post-traumatic stress disorder, the symptoms must not be caused by medication, substance abuse or any other illness).

There are powerful arguments for and against diagnosis and categorical labelling of distress in this way. The diagnosis debate is complex, and given that clinical psychologists are trained to deal with complexity, many will not adopt polarized views of diagnosis, instead understanding that it can have positive and negative aspects depending on the context.

Whatever the perspective on diagnosis, it is very difficult to step away from it because diagnosis is ingrained in the language and approach used in services, and thus in clinical psychologists' work in research and practice. It is also a common language within professional networks and wider society and can be the key to a door to support for many people.

Social GRACES and intersectionality

The social GRACES framework (Roper-Hall 1998) has been developed to help consider different and intersecting identities. Aspects of people's identities (such as their physical health) will interact with the social context (e.g. if you do not rely on aids to move, you are less disadvantaged by society, its constructs and surroundings). Identities are an important consideration for the clinical psychologist. The social GRACES have continued to grow in number and a 2012 paper (Burnham 2012) identified 15:

- gender
- geography
- race
- religion
- age
- ability
- appearance
- culture
- class/caste
- education
- employment
- ethnicity
- spirituality
- sexuality
- sexual orientation.

All of these identities apply to all human beings, though some may be more centred than others (i.e. seen as the norm). This can mean something like culture is considered to belong to minoritized groups rather than culture being something everyone has. In addition, some societies or cultures may hold other aspects of identity not on this list as valuable, or not consider some of those on the list relevant.

The social GRACES can be visible or invisible. For example, racialized identity is often visual, but sexuality less so.

Social GRACES can be voiced or unvoiced. For example, people may conceal their sexuality.

As well as thinking about the identities of those they work with, an important part of clinical psychologists' work is to reflect on their own identities in relation to them. This can feel difficult for those with more privileged identities where acknowledging relative advantage challenges beliefs about things like their career success being due to merit, the idea that it is hard work alone that leads to success in the world.

These identities intersect and overlap, meaning that people who experience greater social disadvantage because of a particular identity can be further impacted if another of their identities is also socially disadvantaged. Alternatively, someone may be disadvantaged in one aspect of their identity but privileged in another (e.g. a white gay man may hold more social power than a black lesbian woman). The concept of intersectionality is therefore an important consideration for clinical psychologists during assessment and formulation, and throughout their work.

Motivational interviewing

Motivational interviewing (MI) is a technique used to help people move towards change, especially when there is resistance or ambivalence. Clinical psychologists may apply the models and tools in their work in different ways (e.g. with a teenager who is struggling with anxiety but not ready to engage in therapeutic work that may be helpful). One of the underpinning frameworks in MI is DiClemente and Prochaska's Stages of Change model (DiClemente and Velasquez 2002). This outlines five stages that people may experience when moving towards change and include: pre-contemplation, contemplation, preparation, action and maintenance. Relapse is often added because it is recognized that this can be part of a process of long-term change.

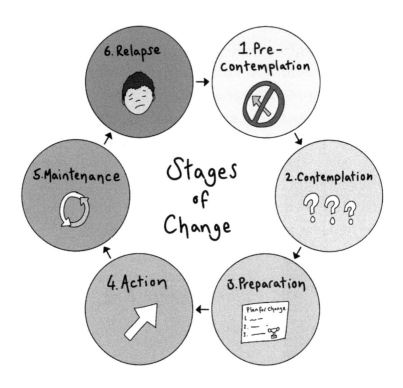

Motivational interviewing can be considered as comprising four steps:

1. engaging the client/patient and practitioner in the development of shared trust and rapport

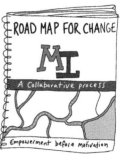

2. focusing on the unwanted or negative behaviour that the person wants or needs to change

3. evoking the rationale for change (i.e. the motivating factors and which ones might be the strongest or most important to the person)

KEY CLINICAL PSYCHOLOGIST SKILLS AND TOOLS

4. planning by the client/patient (supported by the practitioner) to develop their own road map for change, acknowledging where they currently are in that journey, and what steps are needed to achieve their desired change.

Evaluation and measuring impact overview

One of the ways clinical psychologists can apply their scientist-practitioner skills is by collecting data to measure outcomes of intervention and evaluate the impact of their work. This might be done by collecting quantitative data using standardized measures which have been developed through research. They are said to be a valid and reliable way to capture the core aspects of a phenomenon (e.g. anxiety) for individuals who have shared characteristics with the original research cohort. A clinical psychologist might use such tools during assessments and for charting change over time. This can offer an insight into whether the work they are doing is having an impact – with individuals or systems.

Idiographic measures are also valuable tools; they are designed and used to fit specific needs, communication styles or issues. They are most helpful where existing and tested standardized measures do not exist or do not meet the needs of a particular person/system, situation or issue. An example might be a thermometer chart to measure anger on a daily basis. Qualitative data, such as verbal feedback on what changes the intervention has made to a person's life, is also extremely important alongside these more structured methods.

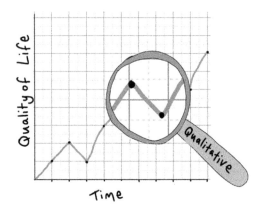

The data from these standardized and ideographic measures and qualitative feedback can come directly from the people the psychologist is working with (self-report), from others (e.g. family members, teachers, support workers) and from observations (e.g. by psychologists). Sometimes, data gathered can be conflicting; it is the job of the scientist-practitioner clinical psychologist to use their skills, knowledge and training to try to help make sense of this.

This is especially important where there is limited evidence for the effectiveness of certain measures to capture what they are supposed to. Even when using interpreters, some terminology used in measures will not directly translate (e.g. there is no word for anxiety in Gujarati), leaving it up to the psychologist or translator to define them, inevitably leading to ambiguity. Many standardized measures have a long way to go before they have stronger reliability and validity for the populations that psychologists are working with.

Teaching and training

Clinical psychologists teach and train others in academic and clinical settings. In academia, it is perhaps obvious that clinical psychologists train those studying clinical psychology at undergraduate and postgraduate levels, but clinical psychologists' expertise in systems thinking, leadership, social psychology, and so on, also contributes to them training medical, business and sports students (among others). Some clinical psychologists work exclusively in academia, working on research to push forward psychological understanding and theory development.

In a clinical setting, it might be clinical psychologists' knowledge of mental health, risk, staff wellbeing, supervision and reflection that they share with others through training. This might include topics such as motivational interviewing, having difficult conversations and trauma-informed care.

Clinical psychologists use their understanding of psychology – how people learn and process information, and how they might respond to difficult or stressful situations – to improve learning environments. For example, people who have autism can find education settings very stressful or find that their autism-related coping strategies make it difficult to get the most out of education at any level. A clinical psychologist can use their understanding of autism to inform and developed an autism-informed learning environment to best support people to strive to thrive in educational settings.

CHAPTER 4

What Are the Main Therapy Approaches Clinical Psychologists Use?

This chapter focuses on key therapeutic approaches that clinical psychologists are trained in and use in clinical practice. Therapeutic approaches can take many years of specific training and closely supervised practice for a practitioner to develop proficiency, and it can be unethical to use them without training. The following overviews are simplistic snapshots of complex theoretical ideas and approaches, and only those who undertake appropriate training, have appropriate supervision, qualifications and/or accreditations should provide such therapies. Professional bodies regulate the profession and provide accessible lists of qualified individuals. This is to avoid harm from those not appropriately trained or supervised.

Cognitive behavioural therapy

Cognitive behavioural therapy (CBT) has two main underlying influences: behavioural therapy and cognitive therapy (e.g. Beck 1964, 1979). Over the decades, areas of the cognitive and behavioural approaches influenced each other to such an extent that they grew into what we now know as CBT.

CBT approaches are based on the concept that thoughts, feelings, physical sensations and behaviours are all interlinked; by changing one we can influence the others and break cycles that maintain distress. Cognitions (thoughts, beliefs, images, etc.) are considered to influence how we emotionally and behaviourally react; how people perceive an experience, interpret it and what it means to them will be different. In therapy, the therapist and client will collaboratively explore thinking patterns and beliefs that are proving problematic. They can then look for and test out alternatives, leading to emotional and behavioural response change. Similarly, CBT may focus on changing behaviours, to make them less 'maladaptive' or less likely to reinforce negative cycles; this in turn helps to reduce negative cognitions and emotions.

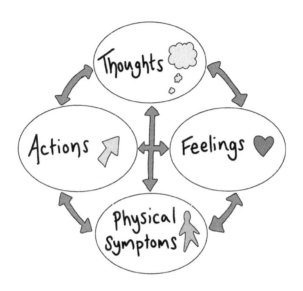

CBT is a collection of therapeutic approaches that can be used in one-to-one work or with groups. It predominantly focuses on what is happening in the here and now to maintain a person's difficulties, rather than focusing on what started or triggered them in the first place. However, CBT does not ignore the past, as this can provide vital clues to the here and now. A CBT practitioner may work on past events to help the client move forward, where their difficulties are particularly long-standing and complex. CBT done well takes account of systemic factors or influences, and individual backgrounds, beliefs and identities.

CBT is a short-term therapeutic intervention, often between six and 20 one-hour sessions. However, a lot of the 'work' happens between therapy sessions, with clients expected to do 'homework' (e.g. keeping diaries and testing out what they have learned in therapy). The aim of CBT is to develop the client's understanding, skills and tools to identify and reduce vicious cycles that maintain difficulties for them. Endings, continuing progress, relapse prevention and future goals are therefore important considerations in CBT.

Many CBT interventions have been manualized to provided standardized treatments based on the evidence base. However, applied skilfully, CBT can be also be tailored to the individual's needs. Unfortunately, assumptions made about the approach can mean that people with more complex needs (e.g. learning disabilities) can often miss out on being offered effective CBT. This is despite there being evidence to show that it could help with these groups.

Narrative exposure therapy

Narrative exposure therapy (NET) is a method of trauma processing for those impacted by multiple traumatic events across their lifeline. Developed by Schauer, Neuner and Elbert (2011) as a short-term intervention for children and adults who continue to be impacted by the legacy of significantly traumatic events, it is often used with those affected by war and conflict. It aims to process and contextualize traumatic events within a whole-life narrative.

NET is built on the premise that overwhelming traumatic events have triggered emotions, physical sensations and cognitions that are easily activated when reminded of the trauma. These are known as 'hot' memories and come to dominate a person's narrative over existing 'cold' memories (those that are not loaded with trauma responses) and need to be recontextualized to reduce their effect. By working through someone's life narrative and slowing down to process the trauma memories, hot memories can become cold.

NET starts with building safety through the therapeutic relationship and psychoeducation into the assumptions of the model to normalize and legitimize the person's trauma responses. Following this, the entire 'lifeline' is laid out as a one-session activity. This involves using a ribbon to signify the person's life and then laying items along the line to represent different events in that life, typically with flowers representing positive events and stones representing negative and traumatic ones. Candles can be used to represent when someone has died, and other items, such as sticks, can be used to represent when the person has hurt another.

Subsequent sessions involve starting at birth and moving quickly through the cold memories and then in more detail through the hot memories. The therapist will start by asking for detail from just before the trauma (e.g. What could you see, hear, smell?) before working through the trauma memory by slowly eliciting detailed sensory information. The therapist needs to be tuned in and compassionate and ensure a pendulation between the past trauma memory and the here and now. The therapist will be keeping a detailed narrative that will be read back to the person at the end of the therapy.

Acceptance and commitment therapy

Acceptance and commitment therapy (ACT) is a behavioural therapy based on relational frame theory, a complex theory of human language and cognition, which is not covered here. The approach relates to the skill of accepting what is not in your control, and taking committed actions towards living a life of value. It can be used by clinical psychologists in many different areas, particularly where external factors contributing to distress are not within the person's immediate control (e.g. a life-limiting health condition). ACT is often referred to as a 'third wave' CBT approach.

Acceptance in ACT is seen as an active choice, providing the client with an alternative to their understandable response of avoiding difficult experiences and feelings. The client accepts that pain and suffering are a part of experience. Cognitive defusion is a technique designed to help  the person take a step back from their thoughts, and not get automatically fixated and tangled up with them. Being present uses tools like mindfulness (from Eastern philosophies) to bring awareness to the present moment, without attempting to change it.

One aim of ACT is to help identify someone's core values and then for them to work towards acting/living according to these values. Values are the ideals or concepts that are central to what we hold as important and what are key to our living what we see as a fulfilled life. Committed action is making an active choice to turn towards, not away from, these values, even in the face of fear, pain and discomfort.

One critique of ACT is that, facilitated by untrained

individuals, it risks invalidating people's pain and suffering. A clinical psychologist using ACT or ACT principles will need to carefully combine it with skills that communicate validation and empathy. This is part of the clinical art referred to in other parts of this book.

Dialectical behaviour therapy

Dialectical behaviour therapy (DBT) was developed in the 20th century by Marsha Linehan (Linehan and Wilks 2015). DBT draws from cognitive behavioural therapy and is often termed a 'third wave' CBT approach. It builds on core CBT tools combined with Eastern philosophies and techniques of mindfulness, acceptance and distress tolerance. It was developed to help people understand the triggers for intense emotional and cognitive experiences and learn to regulate them to help avoid undesired and sometimes dangerous reactions.

The DBT therapist validates and accept the client's thoughts and feelings at the time, while also giving them alternatives that might work better for them in general. They work together to build a 'tool kit', equipping the person with new skills and supporting them to change.  Behaviours that might act as a barrier to therapy (e.g. avoidance and not attending therapy), as well as suicidal and self-harming behaviour can often be the target for DBT work. Some DBT interventions are supported by crisis telephone coaching

In DBT, mindfulness underpins the approach and supports people to bring awareness and can build acceptance and distress tolerance. Acceptance is used by the therapist to support the client to accept the reality of how things are, and why they do what they do. Distress tolerance supports a client to get through a period of heightened emotional pressure, without impulsively reacting. Being able to sit with and tolerate very distressing feelings can help people to make an informed choice about how to respond. There can be aspects of rethinking difficult experiences to reduce strong emotional reactions. Interpersonal effectiveness skill development in DBT helps the client then use all the skills learned in therapy to strengthen and build positive connections with others.

Criticism exists around DBT in that it can be seen as invalidating what are understandable and normal responses to trauma or disempowerment. It takes skill in the clinical psychologist to ensure people feel validated, while also supporting them to change.

Compassion-focused therapy

Compassion-focused therapy (CFT) is an approach to mental wellness aimed at developing internalized self-compassion within individuals. Developed by Paul Gilbert (2009), it draws on evolutionary psychology, cognitive behavioural therapy, Buddhist principles, developmental psychology and neuroscience. The approach is grounded in the concept of internal 'systems' that humans operate in. These include: the drive system, associated with dopamine and task completion; the soothe system, associated with opiates, oxytocin, stress management and bonding with others; and the threat system, aimed at protecting us and associated with adrenalin. All these systems are needed for survival, but an imbalance can lead to difficulties with stress and mental health issues. One of the aims of CFT is to bring awareness to these systems so the person can find balance between them.

One of the primary aims in therapy is for the person to develop compassion towards themselves and others. This is done through exercises and training, including distress tolerance, mindfulness, compassionate imagery and appreciation exercises.

Clinical psychologists may follow a CFT intervention or integrate elements into other approaches. It can be particularly helpful for those who have high levels of self-criticism or low self-esteem. Some people may find self-compassion too alien and uncomfortable, which requires a skilled approach by the psychologist to bring in elements of CFT into other therapy modalities.

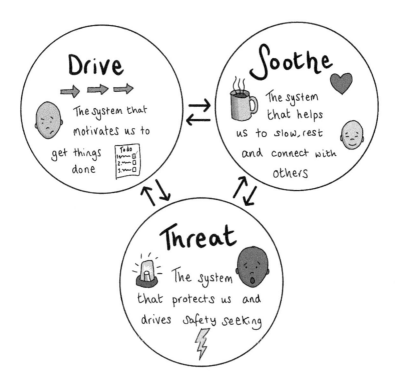

Cognitive analytic therapy

Cognitive analytic therapy (CAT) is a relational-based, time-limited therapy developed in the 1980s by Dr Anthony Ryle (Leiman 1994). It combines psychoanalytic and cognitive theories (among others) and is aimed at addressing a range of problems, including complex relational issues. It provides a framework for therapy but is flexible and has an emphasis of working alongside rather than 'doing to'.

CAT aims to explore patterns of coping in relationships that developed early in life but are now maladaptive. The therapist will work in a non-judgemental and relationally focused way to help people to see how behaviour may be limiting life experiences and continuing negative patterns of relating. One of the key concepts in CAT is reciprocal roles. This is based on the idea that how we are treated early in life leads to our view of ourselves, the world and others. An example of this would be the critical/criticized role: the person who has experienced persistent criticism creates an internalized parent who is critical and a view of oneself as the criticized. This subconscious internalization can lead to behaviour responses that in turn fulfil the belief.

The strategies people have developed are conceptualized as target problem procedures (TPP). These maladaptive patterns are known as traps, dilemmas and snags and are mapped out collaboratively in therapy for both therapist and client to understand more. An example of a TPP might be when a person has experienced neglect and where the reciprocal roles could therefore be 'neglecting' and 'being ignored'. The behaviour the person engages in may be self-neglect via not maintaining relationships which then results in feelings of being ignored by others.

This mapping out is captured in a 'reformulation letter' and can lead to a new understanding of the difficulties and underpin new ways of the person respond- ing to the world. The therapeutic relationship or current life exam-  ples may be used to explore examples of traps, dilemmas and snags. The person is then supported to develop new ways of thinking, feeling and behaving.

Unlike other therapies based on psychoanalytic principles, CAT is time-limited and therefore endings are known in advance. The therapist must be sensitive to past losses and the challenges of not being able to 'fix' everything. At the end an in-depth structured goodbye letter is written from the therapist to the client. Follow-up happens at three months or more and allows evaluation of the work but also consolidation for the client.

Dyadic developmental psychotherapy

Dyadic developmental psychotherapy (DDP) is an approach developed by Daniel Hughes to help the relationship dyad between a child and their primary caregivers (Hughes 2006). Often used when early attachment trauma has been experienced, the approach is commonly used with adoptive parents and their children. When people have experienced traumatic early relationships, this can lead to distrust in parents and adaptive ways of being that can challenge parents and other caregivers. The aim of DDP is for the therapist to work alongside the parent–child relationship to offer the child a therapeutic, safe and attuned parental experience that allows the child to feel less anxious and less need to get control.

DDP principles can be applied to child–parent dyads, but also in teams and systems. In the child–adult set up, a clinical psychologist trained in DDP might first work with the parent on their own before bringing the child in to therapy. They will then work to foster an approach with the child known as PACE (playfulness, acceptance, curiosity and empathy), which is a cornerstone of DDP.

DDP principles can be used in teams around children. This may be in therapeutic environments such as residential placements where there are multiple caregivers. Mirroring PACE, clinical psychologists may offer a space to think about the challenges that children with early relationship trauma bring and offer guidance on how to respond in a therapeutic way to build trust in the adults around them.

Systemic and family therapy

Systemic therapy is not family therapy, but therapists who work with families and couples often use systemic therapy and call themselves family or couple therapists. However, systemic therapy can also be used with individuals and staff teams.

At the centre of systemic therapy is the idea that everyone is part of a system and that to understand an individual we need to also understand the system around them – which might be their family, their work environment, their peer group or wider system issues, such as culture, gender norms, etc. These systems are made up of interconnected and interdependent parts, and changes in one part of the system will impact on others. A useful metaphor to visualize this is a baby's cot mobile, if one piece is tugged, the rest of the 'system' and pieces move.

A systemic therapist will work alongside people to co-create new ways to view and act within their systems. There are a number of 'schools' within systemic therapy, and each has its own way of viewing the problem and how a systemic therapist might help. The main schools in use today are post-Milan therapy  and structural therapy, but many systemic therapists use a combination of techniques drawn from different schools. These include solution-focused and narrative therapy (both of which are covered later), which are not based on systems theory and so not strictly 'systemic', but which do work with people to consider the environments that surround them which either limit or enable their lives.

Post-Milan therapy considers the contexts that influence the system, as well as the beliefs held in the system that maintain stuck patterns of relating. Therapy involves hypothesizing how the problem is being maintained by the system and asking questions aimed at changing dynamics; change is led by the family and is not prescribed by the therapist. The post-Milan school developed working with reflecting teams because it was seen that the therapist is part of the system and therefore reflections offered on this can be helpful. Structural therapy assumes families work best in hierarchical structures with clear roles and responsibilities. Therapy focuses on changing behaviour in the system to re-create and reinforce healthier structures and hierarchies. Early forms of structural therapy took an expert position on what hierarchies should look like, but modern forms of this therapy take account of cultural variation.

Systemic therapy always keeps the system in mind and measures change in relation to the whole system, as it is only through the whole system shifting that new ways of being together and living can be maintained. This is why multiple members of the system are often invited to therapy, which at the start of therapy can be challenging for a family who may only see one of their members as being 'the problem'. The therapist must therefore work skilfully to avoid blame and shame and help the family recognize how they all have a part to play in how any one of their members is doing. When working systemically with individuals, the wider system is still 'brought into the room' through questions, or the therapist might reach out to the system beyond the client in the room by setting the client homework exercises that involve other people, or even using techniques such as writing letters with the client to share their successes with others.

Clinical psychologists may draw on systemic approaches and theory in other elements of their work. They might draw out a family tree known as a genogram that can aid understanding of the systems around someone. Bronfenbrenner's ecological systems theory (1979) is also a useful theory to apply to thinking about the system. Systemic therapy can be done with families, but also with one person and with larger systems such as mental health teams.

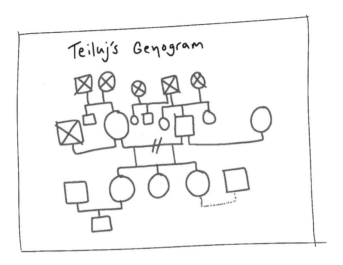

Narrative approaches

All humans try to make sense of what is going on around them and make meaning of events across time through linking them together. Narrative therapists would call the meaning that is made the 'plot' of a story, as the story organizes and maintains the meaning. The same event might have multiple stories told about it; some of these stories are helpful and enabling, others are unhelpful and oppressing. Some stories are dominant, but underneath there are always subjugated stories, so that if the dominant story is oppressive, the subjugated stories might provide an alternative meaning that is enabling.

For example, a child might overhear a story told about

them that they are shy and sensitive, and as a result enter their adult life withdrawn and unsure of themselves. However, beneath this dominant story, there might be an alternative story that they are great at empathy and compassion. Embracing this subjugated story might mean the young adult harnesses their 'strengths', which had previously been storied as limitations, and train to become a successful therapist.

All stories exist within wider contexts. These might be of culture, gender, age, class, and so on, and this will also influence how a story is told. For example, a particular behaviour in a woman might be seen as aggressive and so discouraged, whereas in a man the same behaviour might be considered ambitious and applauded. Exploring the contexts in which people live and which influence their stories is a way that narrative therapists deconstruct stories.

A narrative therapist will look for 'unique outcomes', as

there are always contradictions to a dominant story; for example, the only way you know you are sad is because you must have once been happy. The problem-saturated story with which a person arrives in therapy, is often a 'thin description' of them. A narrative therapist explores more helpful and enabling stories, and when these are found, the therapist helps 'thicken the plot' by hearing more about them, maybe evening bringing in others to strengthen the emerging story either through practices such as letter writing or awarding certificates, or through inviting in 'outsider witness groups' to hear and celebrate the new story.

Because narrative therapists believe that there is no essential truth, a person is never seen as being the problem; the problem is the problem (White and Epston 1989). This fundamental belief allows the problem to be 'externalized' and explored to help the client find those unique outcomes and times when they are different to the dominant story. For example, someone with an eating disorder (which might even be given a name (e.g. Anna anorexia) might be asked questions such as 'When are times when Anna's voice is not so loud?', 'What or who does Anna retreat from?' and 'If Anna were to go on holiday, what would you do differently?'. Questions and techniques such as these can allow the therapist scope to be playful and creative with clients, so that interventions are co-constructed in a way that has deep personal resonance with clients.

Solution-focused therapy

Solution-focused therapy was influenced by an early form of systemic therapy called 'strategic therapy' that is no longer in use, as well as by the work of the American psychiatrist Martin Erikson and Austrian/British philosopher Ludwig Wittgenstein. The Mental Research Institute in the USA also had an influence, with a focus on short-term therapy and behavioural change. The therapy was developed by Insoo Kim Berg and her partner, Steve de Shazer, from the late 1970s onwards (De Jong 2019).

Rather than focus on problems, Solution-focused therapy does just what it says: it focuses on solutions in a goal-orientated way to achieve desired behaviour change. For example, a key technique is 'the miracle question' where a client will be asked 'If you woke up tomorrow and your problem was magically gone, what would you notice was different?'. This is followed by a series of questions to draw out the details of what would be changed (e.g. 'What would be the first thing you did?', 'What would other people notice?'), so that the therapist can look for behaviours and patterns that will help sustain the change towards the desired goal.

A therapist might also ask about how a client is managing to cope and carry on, about previous solutions and about 'exceptions' to the problem, and again, find out in detail what made it possible for things to be different. Therapists will use 'scaling questions', where a client is asked to rate from 1 to 10 where they see themselves now (1  being the worst things have been and 10 being the best they could be). Immediately, the therapist focuses on the next number up on the scale and asks what would be different if the client were there (e.g. a 6 rather than a 5). The client tells the therapist what needs to change, and the therapist helps the client feel motivated and hopeful that they can achieve this change.

The therapy is meant to be brief and so the therapist will ask at the end of each session whether another session is necessary, with an average of six sessions. The therapist listens carefully for even the smallest example of change in the direction outlined by the client, and gives compliments when this is achieved, as well as inviting clients to do homework between sessions to try out the change they wish to see. Solution-focused therapy is used for a variety of problems, particularly in drug addiction and life coaching.

Community psychology

Community psychology is a broad approach that has multiple underpinnings, including social psychology and systems theories. It is often associated with the liberation of marginalized communities and sees this as a vehicle to reduce emotional distress. The location of dysfunction that is leading to poor mental health is placed at the broader systems level rather than that of the individual. This contextual lens links closely with ecological theories (e.g. Bronfenbrenner 1979).

Community psychology might consider the influential systems to be wider than the immediate community and look at the impact of societal narratives and how they play out in power dynamics that contribute to distress.

Interventions might be aimed at changing the conditions of people's lives and challenging dominant societal dynamics and narratives in an empowering way. Several popular metaphors exist to explain the preventive aspect of community psychology approaches, including turning down the taps, rather than mopping the floor, and fixing the bridge rather than rescuing people who are drowning. In practice, working alongside communities and valuing their voice and expertise is privileged over the expertise of the professional. Psychological professionals may bring knowledge and power but are collaborators in intervention rather than leaders. This way of working in the context of disempowering societal dynamics can be understood as an intervention in and of itself.

Within community psychology, individualized interventions can be seen as disempowering because they maintain an expert/user dynamic. However, it is possible to bring in values associated with community psychology to clinical psychologists' work. Participation within services is important for this, and clinical psychologists can work to create openings for people to have a voice about what works for them in service provision. A clinical psychologist may also be working towards systems change by using their psychological understanding to change policy. There can also be a valuing of community resources and space created within therapy to consider strength, resource and voice.

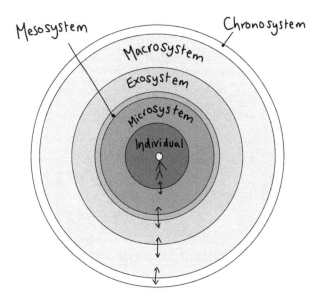

A drawback of community psychology is that it can be difficult to measure and evidence the impact of these ways of working. This is because impacts may be felt over time and in ways that do not fit into standardized measures that align more with scientific methods. It can also require commitment from people and an acceptance that this sort of work can take time. There may also be resistance to these ways of working because they do not have an evidence base that maps neatly onto the quantitative evidence that is so often privileged in commissioning or research studies. Community psychology also requires those familiar with holding a position of power and expertise to relinquish this, which can lead to resistance.

Those clinical psychologists wanting to take on these ways of working therefore need to reflect on how they can do this and where they can find support to ensure they can withstand the challenge. This may require building networks with others working in this way or being creative in how they bring in community psychology values into their work. There is also a fine line to be walked with building an evidence base; one that fits well enough to be trusted with those familiar with more structuralist ways of working, but that also honours the types of evidence that value voice and ways valued by communities.

Clinical neuropsychology

Neuropsychology services employ clinical psychologists who have gone on to do further training in neuropsychology; this could be specializing in adult or child work. Clinical psychologists address concerns with brain, or 'cognitive', functioning; in children these might be about developmental milestones or academic challenges, and in adults they might be about work, social challenges or a decline in functioning in older age. Changes in cognitive functioning might be due to medical, neurological, psychological or genetic causes. Common conditions that neuropsychologists work with include autism, learning and attention disorders such as ADHD, traumatic brain injury, epilepsy, stroke and dementia.

To assess cognitive functioning, clinical neuropsychologists might look at: consciousness, orientation, attention, memory, executive function, language, calculation, perception, behaviour and mood. Relevant history will be taken from multiple sources to guide what to assess. Tests might involve oral questions, computers, paper and pencil, or the manipulation of objects such as puzzles. The findings are analysed and fed back to the person with the concerns and to the people around them, often including recommendations to help overcome the current challenges the person faces.

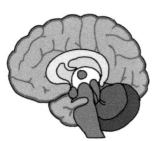

While neuropsychology provides a vital service to children and families, adults and older adults, it has also been criticized as not always being relevant across all cultural and linguistic diversities. The tests used are often not validated with diverse populations and there is often little 'normed' data provided with which to compare scores (Cory 2021). This can lead to health inequalities for those who use neuropsychology services.

Considerations to make when delivering any therapy

Developmental adaptations

Many of the approaches, tools and techniques used by clinical psychologists are applicable across the lifespan if appropriately adapted. Part of the skill of a clinical psychologist is to assimilate information about developmental stages of humans, knowledge about psychological theory and clinical skills. This means that developmental adaptation is a reflexive knitting together rather than a prescriptive action, making it difficult to discuss how it is done. However, there are some examples of how to do this that can guide this art.

Having a trusting therapeutic relationship is important regardless of the developmental stage of the person a clinical psychologist is working with. However, there are times and contexts in people's lives where a relationship is more vulnerable and therefore a trusting alliance may need to be prioritized over other aspects of the therapeutic intervention.

Younger children, those with learning disabilities and older adults experiencing cognitive decline may all need developmental adaptations that take account of cognitive ability. A clinical psychologist may underpin an intervention with psychoeducation and socialization to the model they are using. If the person they are working with struggles to process information about this, it will be important to distil the key concepts in a way that makes the therapeutic intervention accessible but still in line with principles of collaboration and openness.

Presenting information with visual scaffolds and punctuation may be an essential way to make it more accessible and is often a key skill when working with children or those with learning disabilities.

Neurodiversity

Humans are neurodiverse, and this is a broad and complex picture with not enough space to even come close to summarizing the topic here. Neurodiversity refers to differences in how people perceive, experience and interact with the world. Neurodiversity is often associated with autism, though it is also related to things like ADHD, dyslexia and sensory-processing difficulties. Clinical psychologists are likely to work with neurodiversity in the context of their own neurodiversity, that of their colleagues or the people they are working with.

The Western world tends to favour those who are not considered neurodivergent, therefore people who experience differences to the 'norm' may experience barriers to living and thriving. However, neurodivergence brings many strengths in the right context. As an example, the characteristics of ADHD that affect distractibility in one setting may lead to someone being able to juggle multiple tasks at once in another setting and excel in their work. There is also a real need in our world for people who are highly attuned to noticing gaps in sequences, a trait often associated with autism (though this will not necessarily be a trait for every autistic person). However, there is still a way to go in making an inclusive and 'neuro-celebratory' world.

When working with neurodiversity in the therapy room, there are many considerations that clinical psychologists may need to make. There is so much diversity within neurodiversity that it would be impossible to include even a brief guide here, but the most important thing is that it is considered and reflected upon in our work. It is also important for a clinical psychologist to be aware of 'masking', a term used to describe how people learn to cover up their neurodiversity because they are aware that being themselves can lead to negative responses from others.

Neurodiversity also needs to be considered through an intersectional lens. Gender differences in presentation can lead to misdiagnosis, especially in women. Neurodiverse characteristics may also be understood differently across cultures, and how traits present  may also differ depending on the person's culture. It is a key task of clinical psychologists to be holding an intersectional lens when it comes to neurodiversity.

Cultural considerations

Culture is inherent in humanity, and when working interpersonally it is key to consider it. Our culture is likely to impact how we relate to someone and how they relate to us. It will be a lens through which we receive therapy and offer it. Culture will also have more practical implications on therapeutic work.

Working in a culturally considerate way is sometimes called 'cultural competence'. However, this term has been met with criticism because to be competent implies a completion point, which is impossible if we consider the diversity of cultures that exist in the world. It is more important for clinical psychologists to demonstrate openness, curiosity and cultural humility. They will need first to reflect on and bring awareness about their own culture and what of this they bring into the therapy space. Those from dominant cultures sometimes see themselves as not having a culture because everyone around them shares theirs. They also need to be mindful of how culture might interact with the therapy process:

- *Relationship to help* (Reder and Fredman 1996): How do you as a therapist assume people will relate to the helper and help dynamic? Do you assume people will give an opinion if you directly ask because your culture does this? Or are you curious about how they may not question or challenge authority figures due to their cultural rules?
- *Times of year*: Perhaps less about culture and more about religion, but can be linked to culture. Do you assume that people will celebrate Christmas? Are you thinking about prayer times when scheduling sessions? Do you keep up to date with cultural or religious festivals that may affect attendance at sessions?

- *Belief systems*: Our belief systems are interlinked with

culture and may be brought into the therapy room. Are you considering how someone's beliefs or faith may play a part in their healing journey and actively respecting and being open to a different way of thinking about a problem?

- *The role of gender and communities*: For some cultures, it would not be okay for a woman to be in a room with a man without a chaperone. There also needs to be a consideration of any community conflicts that may exist within a person's culture. For some, it may be dishonouring of their community to be seen by a clinical psychologist from a certain community.

Clinical psychologists can use supervision, research and curiosity to develop their skills in cultural humility and reflect on their own culture and that of the people they work with.

De-centring Western ideas in the therapy context

As mentioned in other sections of this book, it is important to remember that, in the Western world, psychology research (and therefore theory development) is based on large proportions of research participants being from a white, educated, industrialized, rich and democratic (WEIRD) background. Therefore, these theories, and the practice that develops from them, may not be valid or relevant for all clients. However, clinical psychologists trained in Western universities may only have been exposed to these ideas and supervised to develop their therapeutic practice based on them.

Moving beyond this to embrace more global perspectives and ideas benefits all clients, but clinical psychology students and qualified staff will need to make an effort to find and develop this knowledge. In addition, some ideas currently used in psychology (e.g. The Tree of  Life in narrative therapy, or mindfulness in CBT) originated in non-Western contexts, and it is important to correctly credit where these ideas come from (Tree of Life was created by Ncube (2006) in Zimbabwe, and mindfulness originates in Buddhism).

Endings

How a clinical psychologist works towards ending a therapeutic relationship with a client is a skill. Endings will mean different things to different people but should always be treated with care. It is also important to remember that endings take place within a context, not only the context of the therapeutic relationship, but also how the service where the therapy took place views endings (e.g. a long-term psychoanalytic centre will take a different approach to a relatively short-term CBT service). Endings might be experienced as a loss, as the celebration of a 'cure' (a clean bill of health), as a transition (recognizing that there is no end point to psychological health), as a relief (if the therapy has been hard) or as a metamorphosis (as change) (Fredman and Dalal 1998).

It is therefore useful for the therapist to reflect on both their own view of the ending, and that of the client, and whether these correspond or differ when considering how to discuss the upcoming end of therapy with a client. It is always useful to reflect on learning and growth, but it might also be important to acknowledge loss and ongoing struggles that the client must now manage without the therapist, applying the learning they have gained from the therapy.

CHAPTER 5

Research

Clinical psychologists are both consumers and generators of research as scientist-practitioners. Research is a cornerstone of the profession, a central thread running through many aspects of how a clinical psychologist trains, reflects, practices and supports others. Some clinical psychologists work in academia and research full-time, leading research in their areas of expertise. Research that clinical psychologists draw on can come from academic studies, but it also comes from practice-based evidence and sometimes research conducted by third sector services such as charities. This chapter introduces a range of ways clinical psychologists use and get involved in research.

Ethics in research

Being an ethical researcher means that participants and readers of the research can trust the researcher. The British Psychological Society (2021) provides clear ethical guidelines that outline the conditions that must be in place for ethical research to occur; these are briefly summarized here.

Researchers must respect the autonomy, right to privacy and experience of their participants. All participants must have freely given their consent to take part, and have been given sufficient information to make an informed choice about this – this includes the right to  withdraw from the research at any time without giving a reason. Consent should be carefully documented and renewed if the conditions change under which consent was originally given. Information about participants must be kept confidential unless agreed in advance, and participant identities should be anonymized.

Researchers have a responsibility to conduct research with integrity and of high quality that maximizes benefit and minimizes harm, paying particular attention to any risk factors (e.g. invasive procedures, recruiting vulnerable people, etc.). Research recruiting children and young people under 16 years needs special consideration (see BPS 2021 for more details). Research should always go through an ethical review process, with details of this described in the research write-up.

There is more to ethical research than the considerations provided by the BPS. Researchers have a social responsibility and need to consider who might gain or lose from their research: whose voices are heard over others; which communities benefit; could the research question be asked differently to advance those usually oppressed or ignored? For example, Roberts *et al.* (2020) found that 'race' is rarely mentioned in psychological research, that most journal editors are white and that when race is written about, the majority of the first authors of these papers are also white – this is not about the quality of the research but about structural racism.

WEIRD research

A critique of psychology research is that it is primarily carried out with people from Western, educated, industrialized, rich and democratic (WEIRD) societies. This is because a significant proportion of empirical studies of human psychological behaviour is conducted with white college students in North America. However, WEIRD populations make up only 12 per cent of the world's population, and assuming findings from studies are generalizable for the other 88 per cent is problematic. Added to this, WEIRD research participants may be psychological outliers, further reinforcing how concerning their dominance in psychological research is (Henrich, Heine and Norenzayan 2010).

This is a significant issue for the clinical psychology profession because it is underpinned by this limited evidence base. National Institute for Health and Care Excellence (NICE) guidance that informs training courses and clinical intervention practice in the UK is relied on as generalizable to the populations clinical psychologists are working with. However, it is important that clinical psychologists remain critical about the evidence base on which these guidelines are formed, especially when working with diverse populations.

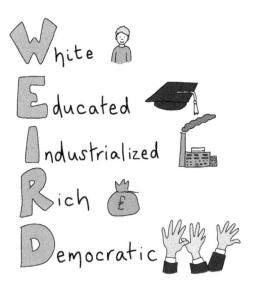

Quantitative research

Quantitative means numbers, so quantitative research focuses on the collection, analysis and reporting of data in numerical form. Often, quantitative research aims to collect large amounts of data in a systematic way that can be analysed to identify patterns, test hypotheses (theories), establish the significance of differences and similarities, and/or to create generalizable findings and conclusions to larger populations, settings and phenomena.

Quantitative data can be generated using a number of research methodologies, such as questionnaires, surveys, observations and experimental design. Quantitative researchers also use existing datasets, like the data routinely collected in mental health services, to look at them in new/different ways. This is known as secondary data analysis.

Quantitative data can be ana-lysed and reported simply using descriptive statistics (such as range, mean, percentages) through data tables, graphs and figures. However, clinical psychologists are also trained to use more advanced sta-tistics and packages. Quantitative research can be done in isolation, or in sequence, parallel with or truly integrated with qualitative research; the latter is known as mixed-methods research.

In quantitative research, the concepts of reliability and validity are important to indicate the quality of the research. Reliability refers to whether a finding can be reproduced if the research is conducted again in the same conditions. Reliable results are expected to remain the same across time (test-retest reliability), across different researchers (inter-rater reliability) and/or in different parts of the test (internal consistency). Reliability is helped if the research method is applied consistently in a standardized way. Validity refers to whether the tests are measuring what they claim to measure. This could be:

- whether they appear to measure what is claimed to be measured (face validity)
- whether the tests fit with the 'construct', knowledge or theory they are designed to measure (construct validity)
- whether all aspects of this construct are covered (content validity)
- whether the measures align with other valid measures of the same subject (criterion validity)
- whether the results are generalizable (external validity)
- whether the design of the research is robust (internal validity).

There are further sub-sections of these types of validity that we will not go into here. Validity is helped by careful consideration of the selection of measures and participants.

Qualitative research

Qualitative research is used to understand and explore something, not to objectively measure a truth and make a prediction. An important consideration when thinking about research is epistemology and ontology: epistemology is how we know things and ontology is what can be known. It is important to know what epistemological and ontological position will be taken when planning what research to do. Within qualitative research, different positions can be taken along these lines depending on the research question, which will align to the assumptions about how something can be known and what it is possible to know. If doing mixed-methods research, using both qualitative and quantitative research methods, it is important that the epistemological positions of the two methods align.

There is a continuum of epistemological positions, with realism at one end and relativism at the other:

- *Realist position*: Data provides information about how things really are in the world. Methods should elicit true and undistorted representations.
- *Relativist position*: 'Pure' experience does not exist, cultural and discursive resources construct different versions of experience. Methods need to identify and unpack such resources.

Similarly, ontology can also be considered along a continuum, with positivism at one end and constructivism at the other:

- *Positivism* considers the world to exist as external to the social actors within it. And so there is a 'reality' out there to be objectively discovered.
- *Constructivism* considers that social actors create their own reality through perception and the actions they take. Thus, there are multiple realities based on subjectivity, and these can change.

Some of the different qualitative approaches to research are included in the image below. A qualitative research or psychology research textbook will give more details about each one than we can here. However, it is worth noting that thematic analysis can be used from any epistemological position, and that there are two types of grounded theory based on different epistemological positions. Phenomenological methods include methods such as interpretative phenomenological analysis, and discursive methods include methods such as narrative analysis, conversation analysis and discourse analysis (of which there are a few).

These methods all have in common that the 'data' are words and not numbers. To get the data, qualitative research will either analyse existing texts (e.g. newspapers) or create text (aka a transcript) through methods such as interviews, focus groups or surveys.

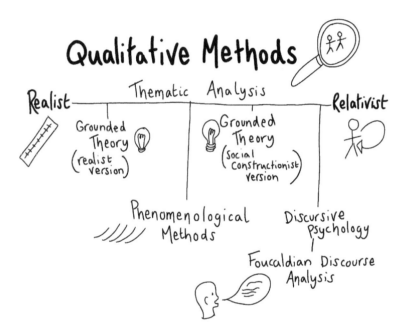

When it comes to the concepts of 'validity and reliability', the evaluation criteria used will need to be compatible with the epistemological position taken. All qualitative research considers the role of the researcher in generating and analysing the data; however, rather than try to remove this, it is instead made transparent as it cannot ever be removed. Rather than the research needing to be 'reliable and valid', by recognizing the role of the researcher it is acknowledged that the exact same results would not be found if someone else did the research again, it is instead important that the research is trustworthy. There are various ways that a researcher can ensure this, including:

- disclosing their values and assumptions and reflecting on their role in shaping the research
- describing who their participants are and whether they are representative of the population in which they are considered
- providing participant quotes for every statement made about the data
- providing credibility checks (e.g. asking participants if the results make sense, running them past an expert in the field, etc.)
- ensuring that a data-based cohort story is created by the researcher, as judged by the reader.

Literature reviews

To build on knowledge within any area, it is important to understand the research already in existence, and the gaps. In research, reviewing the literature is an important part of scene-setting and is often done by knitting together past relevant history, theory and the evidence base to give an overview of an area and to build the context for the piece of work being undertaken or written about. Within clinical psychology research, literature reviews are an important part of contextualizing studies, whether this be in single-case experimental design studies or within randomized control trials. Many of these reviews survey the literature in a non-systematized way, but the most robust form of literature review is considered to be a systematic one.

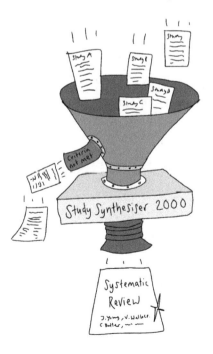

Systematic reviews provide an up-to-date synthesis of all the research available within a specified area. The method is pre-planned and will follow a similar structure to this:

- pilot searches
- defining search terms
- defining inclusion and exclusion criteria
- running the searches on multiple journal databases (and other sources for grey literature, i.e., materials and research produced not produced by traditional commercial or academic publishing)
- abstract screening
- full-text screening
- data extraction
- analysis
- write-up.

Systematic reviews synthesize findings from both qualitative and quantitative studies and the outcomes are seen as being more robust than those of single studies.

Clinical trials

Clinical trials are a form of research that clinical psychologists may be involved in that aim to develop new or improved ways to assess and treat mental health issues. Typically, a clinical trial will be testing something, or way of doing something, that is not yet readily available. This could be a new treatment approach or an existing treatment but with a new population. The primary aim is to establish if it is safe and effective, in comparison to the available alternatives (or no intervention at all). Clinical trials will also be looking for potential unintended consequences and risks.

Due to the novelty of the clinical tools, techniques, equipment, medications or approaches that are being tested, clinical trials must be carefully designed and monitored according to strict guidelines and protocols. 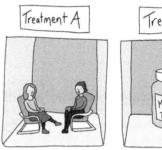 Informed consent for clinical trials is exceptionally important as they are not free from risk, given that they are often testing an unknown situation. Clinical trials tend to generate a lot of data to ensure as much is known about what is being tested as possible.

There are limitations in clinical trials in that they often assume homogeneity. All people will have multiple intersecting differences even when matched against people with similar characteristics. When using clinical trials to look at therapies, there is also an assumption that therapists will be delivering the same intervention. However, we know that therapeutic alliance is a highly powerful factor in therapeutic outcomes and skills to build this will vary across therapists.

Service and quality improvement

Clinical psychologists often use their research training and clinical knowledge to undertake and lead service and quality improvement projects. These often use systematic methods and tools, drawing on a range of research methodologies. Quality and service improvement projects can be small-scale and local, large pieces of work affecting many services, or national programmes (e.g. national audits of mental health in the UK). They can improve the safety, effectiveness, acceptability, cost-efficiency and experience of healthcare (though sometimes these things are in contention with each other). Quality and service improvement can take the form of clinical audit, service evaluation, and pilot or trial development and implementation of new techniques or ways of working.

Quality and service improvement projects may include training of staff, using routinely collected data to improve clinical interventions, and collecting information on the needs and experiences of the service users and staff. One aim of this type of work is to connect those that use healthcare services with those that provide it, to better understand, help, develop and evaluate policy and practice improvements for the benefit of service users, staff, organizations and populations on the whole.

Case studies

A case study is an exploration of a psychological assessment or a piece of psychological therapy work with an individual or with a group. Case studies have formed the basis of many psychological theories and therapeutic approaches and can be a vital way to make sense of, narrate and communicate the idiosyncrasies of personal experience and psychological work. Case studies can be helpful for understanding what works for reporting novel approaches that are yet to be tested in larger-scale research. They also aid practising clinicians to feed real-world clinical psychology practice into the literature. In clinical psychology training, case studies are typically used to exemplify how therapy is done in practice. Trainees are often assessed on their clinical practice through case study assignments.

Case studies can be wholly qualitative in nature, in the form of a reflective account of what happened in a piece of clinical work. They can also be more quantitative in nature, where numeric data are collected, analysed and reported using tools like clinical rating scales and questionnaires. The data are often collected at assessment, at different time points during therapy and then at the end.

Quasi-experimental case studies will often be testing a hypothesis/theory, based on existing literature and research. There is an attempt to manipulate a factor (e.g. the type of therapy tool used) with a prediction that this will have a particular influence on another (e.g. the success of the therapy in reducing the clients' distressing symptoms). In these case studies, a baseline set of data will be collected before any intervention takes place. The baseline data are compared with the therapy and outcome data to support conclusions about whether the hypothesis/theory that was being tested could be supported or not. Case studies allow us to understand depth within a particular case, but the conclusions that can be drawn from them are considered narrow.

Participatory action research

Participatory action research (PAR) is seen as a socially transformative research approach carried out with rather than on people and communities. It is an active collaborative approach to inquiry and is associated with community psychology. Traditional research is often guided by researcher choices and arguably maintains societal power imbalances by enhancing the status of researchers. In PAR, participants lead on decisions in the research and focus on issues relevant to them and their community. Clinical psychologists facilitating PAR are there to share skills and knowledge and potentially use their status and resources to enable the process.

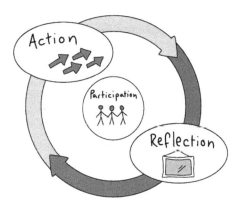

PAR is cyclical, and its oscillation between reflection and action, with its liberatory principles, is strongly aligned with Paulo Freire's (1970) praxis (action and reflection). How many cycles and what PAR actually looks like in practice are not pre-defined, because by nature of the participatory principles it is led by participants. For clinical psychologists to carry out PAR in institutions and mental health services can be challenging, because ethical approval often requires a detailed prediction of what will happen in the project. Because PAR is guided by participants' wants and can be cyclical, it is nearly impossible to predetermine the direction. However, there are types of PAR that allow for PAR within parameters such as photovoice; where participants collect information using cameras and display it in a way that attempts to change something.

Afterword

We set out to write this book to provide an accessible and helpful introductory overview of clinical psychology. Our hope is that it has given those who read it a greater understanding of the profession and has offered a platform from which to build areas of interest. Each section is just a small window onto a much larger body of interesting and detailed research, information and debate. We would recommend using it as a scaffold on which richer knowledge can be explored and grown.

It is important to note that the content included here has been framed by the authors' own experiences, learning and perspectives at a single point in time. During the writing of the book, there was much discussion (and sometimes disagreement) about the angle we were writing from or the content we chose to include. This is perhaps a healthy reflection of the profession and how it can become richer through diversity of thought and perspective. Our hope is that as well as an introduction to clinical psychology, it is also a vehicle to promote discussion and growth; we invite you join us in the ongoing conversation, exploration and development of the profession for the improved lives of all.

References

American Psychiatric Association (2013) *Diagnostic and Statistical Manual of Mental Disorders* (5th edn). Washington, DC: APA.

Bandura, A. (1976) *Social Learning Theory*. Englewood Cliffs, NJ: Prentice Hall.

Barry, M. and Jenkins, R. (2007) *Implementing Mental Health Promotion*. Philadelphia, PA: Elsevier Health Services.

Beck, A.T. (1964) 'Thinking and depression: II. Theory and therapy.' *Archives of General Psychiatry 10*, 6, 561–571.

Beck, A.T. (1979) *Cognitive Therapy and the Emotional Disorders*. New York, NY: Penguin.

Bretherton, I. (1992) 'The origins of attachment theory: John Bowlby and Mary Ainsworth.' *Developmental Psychology 28*, 5, 759–775.

British Psychological Society (2017) *Practice Guidelines* (3rd edn). Leicester: BPS.

British Psychological Society (2019) *Standards for the Accreditation of Doctoral Programmes in Clinical Psychology*. Leicester: BPS.

British Psychological Society (2021) *Code of Human Research Ethics*. Leicester: BPS.

Bronfenbrenner, U. (1979) *The Ecology of Human Development: Experiments by Nature and Design*. Cambridge, MA: Harvard University Press.

Burnham, J. (2012) 'Developments in Social GGRRAAACCEEESSS: Visible–Invisible and Voiced–Unvoiced.' In I. Krause (ed)

Culture and Reflexivity in Systemic Psychotherapy: Mutual Perspectives. London: Karnac.

Ciofalo, N. (2019) *Indigenous Psychologies in an Era of Decolonization*. New York, NY: Springer.

Compton, M.T. and Shim, R.S. (2015) 'The social determinants of mental health.' *Focus 13*, 4, 419–425.

Cory, J.M. (2021) 'White privilege in neuropsychology: An "invisible knapsack" in need of unpacking?' *The Clinical Neuropsychologist 35*, 2, 206–218.

De Jong, P. (2019) 'A brief, informal history of SFBT as told by Steve de Shazer and Insoo Kim Berg.' *Journal of Solution Focused Practices 3*, 1, 5. Accessed on 26/2/2023 at https://digitalscholarship.unlv.edu/journalsfp/vol3/iss1/5

Department of Health (2019) The NHS Long Term Plan. Accessed on 8/2/2023 at www.longtermplan.nhs.uk

DiClemente, C.C. and Velasquez, M.M. (2002) 'Motivational Interviewing and the Stages of Change.' In W.R. Miller and S. Rollnick (eds) *Motivational Interviewing: Preparing People for Change* (2nd edn) (pp.201–216). New York, NY: Guilford Press.

Festinger, L. (1950) 'Informal social communication.' *Psychological Review 57*, 2271–2282.

Fredman, G. and Dalal, C. (1998) 'Ending discourses: Implications for relationship and therapy in action.' *Human Systems: The Journal of Systemic Consultation and Management 9*, 1, 1–13.

Freire, P. (1970) *Pedagogy of the Oppressed*. New York, NY: Continuum.

Gibbs, G. (1988) *Learning by Doing: A Guide to Teaching and Learning Methods*. London: Further Education Unit.

Gilbert, P. (2009) 'Introducing compassion-focused therapy.' Advances in Psychiatric Treatment 15, 3, 199–208.

Haney, C., Banks, W.C. and Zimbardo, P.G. (1973) 'A study of prisoners and guards in a simulated prison.' *Naval Research Review 30*, 4–17.

Henrich, J., Heine, S.J. and Norenzayan, A. (2010). 'The weirdest people in the world?' *Behavioral and Brain Sciences 33*, 2–3, 61–83.

Horvath, A.O., Del Re, A.C., Flückiger, C. and Symonds, D. (2011) 'Alliance in individual psychotherapy.' *Psychotherapy 48*, 1, 9–16.

Hughes, D.A. (2006) *Building the Bonds of Attachment: Awakening Love in Deeply Troubled Children* (2nd edn). Lanham, MD: Jason Aronson.

Johnstone, L. and Boyle, M. (2018) 'The power threat meaning framework: An alternative nondiagnostic conceptual system.' *Journal of Humanistic Psychology.* doi:10.1177/0022167818793289

Kolb, D.A. (2014) *Experiential Learning: Experience as the Source of Learning and Development.* Upper Sable River, NJ: Pearson Education.

Leiman, M. (1994) 'The development of cognitive analytic therapy.' *International Journal of Short-Term Psychotherapy 9*, 2/3, 67–82.

Linehan, M.M. and Wilks, C.R. (2015) 'The course and evolution of dialectical behavior therapy.' *American Journal of Psychotherapy 69*, 2, 97–110.

Macneil, C.A., Hasty, M.K., Conus, P. and Berk, M. (2012) 'Is diagnosis enough to guide interventions in mental health? Using case formulation in clinical practice.' *BMC Medicine 10*, 1–3.

Martin, D.J., Garske, J.P. and Davis, M.K. (2000) 'Relation of the therapeutic alliance with outcome and other variables: A meta-analytic review.' *Journal of Consulting and Clinical Psychology 68*, 3, 438–450.

McGrath, L., Walker, C. and Jones, C. (2016) 'Psychologists against austerity: Mobilising psychology for social change.' *Critical and Radical Social Work 4*, 3, 409–413.

Milgram, S. (1963) 'Behavioral study of obedience.' *Journal of Abnormal and Social Psychology 67*, 371–378.

Ncube, N. (2006) 'The Tree of Life Project: Using narrative ideas in work with vulnerable children in Southern Africa.' *International Journal of Narrative Therapy and Community Work 1*, 3–16.

Padmanabhanunni, A., Jackson, K., Noordien, Z., Pretorius, T.B. and Bouchard, J.-P. (2022) 'Characterizing the nature of professional training and practice of psychologists in South Africa.' *Annales Médico-Psychologiques, Revue Psychiatrique 180*, 4, 360–365.

Rahim, M. and Cooke, A. (2019) 'Should Clinical Psychologists Be Political?' In W. Curvis (ed) *Professional Issues in Clinical Psychology* (pp.81–91). Abingdon: Routledge.

Reder, P. and Fredman, G. (1996) 'The relationship to help: Interacting beliefs about the treatment process.' *Clinical Child Psychology and Psychiatry 1*, 3, 457–467.

Reisman, J.M. (1991) *A History of Clinical Psychology*. London: Hemisphere Publishing.

Roberts, S.O., Bareket-Shavit, C., Dollins, F.A., Goldie, P.D. and Mortenson, E. (2020) 'Racial inequality in psychological research: Trends in the past and recommendations for the future.' *Perspectives on Psychological Science 15*, 6, 1295–1309.

Rogers, C.R. (1965) 'The therapeutic relationship: Recent theory and research.' *Australian Journal of Psychology 17*, 2, 95–108.

Roper-Hall, A. (1998) 'Working Systemically with Older People and Their Families Who Have "Come to Grief".' In P. Sutcliffe, G. Tufnell and U. Cornish (eds) *Working with the Dying and Bereaved: Systemic Approaches to Therapeutic Work*. London: Macmillan

Royal College of Psychiatrists (2009) *Age Discrimination in Mental Health Services: Making Equality a Reality*. Accessed on 8/8/2023 at www.rcpsych.ac.uk/pdf/PS02_2009x.pdf

Ruscio, A.M. and Holohan, D.R. (2006) 'Applying empirically supported treatments to complex cases: Ethical, empirical and practical considerations.' *Clinical Psychology: Science and Practice 13*, 146–162.

Schauer, M., Neuner, F. and Elbert, T. (2011) *Narrative Exposure Therapy: A Short-term Treatment for Traumatic Stress Disorders*. Cambridge, MA: Hogrefe.

Shapiro, M.B. (1967) 'Clinical psychology as an applied science.' *British Journal of Psychiatry 113*, 502, 1039–1042.

Tajfel, H. (1970) 'Experiences in intergroup discrimination.' *Scientific American 223*, 96–102.

Tasca, C., Rapetti, M., Carta, M.G. and Fadda, B. (2012) 'Women and hysteria in the history of mental health.' *Clinical Practice and Epidemiology in Mental Health 8*, 110–119.

Weiner, B. (1986) *An Attributional Theory of Motivation and Emotion.* New York, NY: Springer-Verlag,

Whitaker, R. (2004) *Mad in America: Bad Science, Bad Medicine, and the Enduring Mistreatment of the Mentally Ill.* New York, NY: Basic Books.

White, M. and Epston, D. (1989) *Literate Means to Therapeutic Ends.* Adelaide: Dulwich Centre Publications.

Wood, N. and Patel, N. (2017) 'On addressing "Whiteness" during clinical psychology training.' *South African Journal of Psychology* 47, 3, 280–291. doi:10.1177/0081246317722099

World Health Organization (2014) *Social Determinants of Mental Health.* Accessed on 8/8/2023 at www.who.int/publications/i/item/9789241506809

World Health Organization (2019) *International Classification of Diseases (ICD-11).* Accessed on 6/8/2023 at www.who.int/standards/classifications/classification-of-diseases

Yanos, P. (2018, 2 June) 'The long shadow of the eugenics movement' [Blog post]. *Psychology Today.* Accessed on 8/8/2023 at www.psychologytoday.com/gb/blog/written/201806/the-long-shadow-the-eugenics-movement

Subject Index

Author Index